BOOKS RELATING TO JOHN LOCKE

THOEMMES
REPRINTS

LOGICAL TRACTS

Comprising Observations and Essays
Illustrative of Mr. Locke's
Treatise upon the Human Understanding

Thomas Ludlam

THOEMMES
BRISTOL

KINOKUNIYA
TOKYO

Published by
Thoemmes Press
85 Park Street
Bristol BS1 5PJ

ISBN 1 85506 116 3
Complete set of 8 volumes: ISBN 1 85506 119 8

This is a reprint of the 1790 Edition

Exclusive distribution of this title in Japan by
Kinokuniya Co. Ltd, Tokyo

Publisher's Note

These reprints are taken from original copies of each book. In many cases the condition of those originals is not perfect, pages having suffered from such things as inconsistent printing pressures, show-through from one side of a leaf to the other, the filling in of some letters and characters, unstable, often handmade, paper and the break up of type. The publisher has gone to great lengths to ensure the quality of these reprints but points out that certain characteristics of the original copies will, of necessity, be apparent in reprints thereof.

LOGICAL TRACTS,

COMPRISING

OBSERVATIONS and ESSAYS

ILLUSTRATIVE OF

Mr. LOCKE's TREATISE

UPON THE

HUMAN UNDERSTANDING:

With Occasional Remarks on the Writings of the

TWO SCOTTISH PROFESSORS,

REID AND STEWART,

UPON THE SAME SUBJECT:

AND A PREFACE IN VINDICATION OF

Mr. LOCKE,

AGAINST THE

MISTAKES AND MISREPRESENTATIONS

OF THE LATE.

Mr. MILNER, of HULL,

Dr. HORNE, BISHOP OF NORWICH;

Mr. KETT, FELLOW OF TRINITY COLLEGE, OXFORD;

AND

Dr. NAPLETON, CANON OF HEREFORD.

By THOMAS LUDLAM, M. A.

Cambridge,

PRINTED BY M. WATSON:

FOR J. NICHOLSON, CAMBRIDGE; SOLD ALSO BY RIVINGTONS,
ST. PAUL'S CHURCH YARD, LONDON; COOKE, OXFORD;
AND GREGORY, LEICESTER.

PREFACE.

~~~o~~~

THE following papers were intended for the improvement in the art of reasoning of such young students in divinity as are *able* to read the writings of Mr. Locke, Bishops Butler, Hurd and Warburton, with those of Dr. Balguy, Powell and Ogden : as for all others, whether the admirers of Messrs. Hutchinson, Jones (of Nayland, commonly called Trinity Jones) Romaine, Milner, Overton, Swedenborg, &c. &c. no man who knows what reasoning is, will think of offering any to such, who reject the very foundation of it, *clear* and *precise* ideas : you might as well think of instructing a man in reading who should refuse to learn his alphabet.

Taught to consider the *attainment* of *truth* as a matter of the highest concern to intelligent creatures ; and *that* of religious truth as the most important employment in which men can possibly be engaged, I have ever thought my warmest gratitude due to that Being, through whose kind providence the care of my education was intrufted to Drs. Powell and Balguy, of St. John's College, Cambridge. Men whofe writings have juftified the opinion the world entertained of their abilities. Poffeffed of integrity equal to their abilities, they were much too honeft to follow the ufual practice of the bigoted partizans of particular opinions : they therefore juftly thought it their duty, not to furnifh me with their *own* creed, but to teach me to reafon, and to ufe with propriety and fairnefs, thofe faculties which God had given me. They had fenfe enough to fee, that if they did their duty in this cafe, they could neither be refponfible for the ufe I might make of my faculties, or for the folly, or falfity of the opinions I might embrace : and as far as the truth, or the wifdom of thefe opinions depended upon the quantity of abilities I might poffefs, they knew performance in this re-fpect would be accepted according to what a man hath, and would not be required according to what a man hath not, becaufe the judge of all the earth will do right. It is furely very ftrange that there can be more than one opinion upon this matter, and yet I have heard many of thofe who are called ferious Divines, blame the late Norrifian Lecturer, Dr. Hey, for *not* entertaining any *fixed* opinions himfelf, and for *not* teaching his hearers *any* opini-ons *at all;* and I have heard at leaft an equal num-ber of the fame fort of perfons blame him for en-tertaining *falfe* opinions, or for teaching his hear-ers *fuch.* But fo it is, though proteftants universally agree to reprobate the infallibility of the Pope they universally act, as if all the different denominations of christians were possessed of it. I was however, taught to pay no regard to human authority in matters of opinion, and to consider *that* truth alone to be worth attention, which was supported by *clear* and uncontrovertible reasoning; for when the arguments on both sides are in perfect equilibrium, the matter under consideration cannot *possibly* be of any importance. But though I am far from thinking Mr. Locke, or any man to be infallible, yet in vindicating the character of this great writer, from the aspersions thrown upon it so long after his death; I am but discharging a common duty of humanity, which survivers owe to those who have deserved well of mankind by their literary labours, when they are past the power of appearing in their own defence. It is indeed singular that *all* Mr. Locke's opponents, from Stillingfleet and Edwards, to Kett and Milner, should shew such a decided aversion to the acquisition of *distinct* ideas, and the use of clear reasoning; and it is surely not a little wonderful that those who have been considered as men of real piety should be *dishonest* enough to bring *general* charges, which no man can refute, because no man can discover the points objected to. Of this sort is that brought by Mr. Joseph Milner, in his reply to Gibbon. In p. 154, he tells us, that Mr. Locke led the fashion of introducing a *pompous parade* of *reasoning* into religion: from that time, says Mr. M.

a rational religion has been the cant term of all who profefs to be wifer than others.

With equal truth, honefty, and difcernment, Mr. Kett, in his hiftory, the interpreter of prophecy, brings a like general charge againft Mr. Locke. In vol. iii. p. 17, 18, edit. i. and vol. ii. p. 131, 132 edit. ii. he fays, " that Mr. Locke's writings led to a fcepticifm, eventually hurtful to religion ; and though a loyal fubject, his political writings generated doctrines hurtful to monarchical government, and indeed to civil fociety. The Effay on the Human Underftanding, in itfelf fo profound and ufeful, with a confiderable degree of erroneous theory, as might be expected from a man even of the greateft genius, exploring untrodden, intricate, and arduous paths, brought a greater acceffion to man of knowledge of thofe powers, by which he is peculiarly diftinguifhed, than any book that had ever been written. It tended alfo to fharpen, and invigorate the faculties. But the caution with which it examined different fpecies and degrees of evidence ; a caution right, as far as it merely prevented error, fometimes refufed to admit truth, fought proof of a different kind from that which the nature of the fubject required, doubted wherein the plain judgment of common fenfe, no doubt could exift, and afforded fuppofed data, from whence ingenious men might form the moft vifionary theories."

It has often been obferved, that children can afk queftions, which the wifeft men cannot an-

fwer; it is no lefs true, that perfons, the moft
flightly acquainted with any fubjects, can bring
general accufations, which it may be, no man,
however well acquainted with the fubject can refute. If Mr. Milner, or Mr. Kett had fpecified
particular inftances, upon which thefe very ferious
accufations were founded; fuch charges would then
have had a claim to be confidered as fomething
more than *mere* calumnies. But till Mr. Milner's
admirers bring *proof where* Mr. Locke introduces a
pompous parade of *reafoning* into religion; and till
Mr. K. points out that erroneous theory, which,
he affirms is to be found in a *confiderable degree*,
in the Effay upon the Human Underftanding; till
he fhews *where* Mr. Locke refufes to *admit* truth,
or feeks proof of a *different* kind from that which
the *nature* of the fubject *required* ; till he acquaints
us where Mr. Locke doubted upon fubjects, which
in the plain judgment of common *fenfe*, admitted
of *no* doubt, and till he points out the matters
which afforded data for the theories of vifionary
men, and what thofe writings of Mr. Locke are
which *neceffarily* led to fcepticifm, and infidelity ;
we muft beg to confider Mr. Kett as an encourager
of the prefent fafhionable political flander. For unlefs Mr. Locke's writings *neceffarily* led to fcepticifm, and infidelity, Mr. Locke is no more to be
blamed than the inventors of printing are, for all
the atheiftical, profane, obfcene, and treafonable
books, which have ever iffued from the prefs : by
which this noble invention has proved *eventually*

hurtful, not only to religion, but alſo to civil ſo-
city. Neverthelefs, however warm Mr. Kett's
zeal may be, we truſt, he will not venture to aſſert,
that Mr. Locke ever wrote any thing hoſtile to
limited monarchy, much leſs will Mr. Kett venture to declare, that *he* thinks *deſpotiſm* preferable
to a *free* government.

But let us do Mr. Kett juſtice : all his charges we
believe are not imaginary ; whether he will have
better luck with his *founded*, than with his *un-
founded* charges, will ſoon appear. Mr. Kett ſays,
that Mr. Locke affirms that we have no *certain*
evidence for the exiſtence of any objects, but ourſelves individually, and the Deity.—Mr. Kett cannot mean that Mr. Locke denies the evidence of
ſenſe.

This charge then I ſuppoſe Mr. Kett grounds
upon the firſt, and ſecond ſections of the eleventh
chapter of the fourth book of Mr. Locke's Eſſay.
The knowledge of our (own) being, ſays Mr.
Locke, we have by intuition. The existence of
God, reaſon (arguing from the information of our
ſeveral ſenſes, Rom. i. 20.) clearly makes known
to us. The knowledge of the exiſtence of all other
things we receive only by *actual* ſenſation. Had
Mr. Kett attended more cloſely to Mr. Locke's
meaning, or had he more clearly underſtood his
own, he would never have brought this objection.

The knowledge men are in *general*, and *uſually*
poſſeſſed of, ariſes from the exertion of our powers,
either of perception, or ſenſation. By our powers

of perception I underſtand thoſe internal faculties of the mind, through whoſe action we are conſcious of our own exiſtence ; and by whoſe action we become acquainted with the relations between our ideas ; whether ſuch relations are diſcoverable, *immediately* and *intuitively*, or *mediately*, that is, by the interpoſition of other ideas. By the powers of ſenſation, I underſtand thoſe corporeal faculties by which we become acquainted with the works of nature, that is, with the different objects of the material world, and the reſpective effects of theſe objects upon each other, and alſo upon ourſelves. Now the action of theſe powers of ſenſe is confined to our own perſonal preſence ; we can receive no information from them reſpecting any objects exiſting, or reſpecting the effects produced by ſuch objects, in places from which we are abſent ; and therefore all the proof we can have of the exiſtence and reality of the material world, is confined to the *ſmall* reach of our bodily ſenſes (I conſider not now the trifling aſſiſtance they can receive from art.) Nothing ſo certain as that it is utterly impoſſible that we can have the teſtimony of our ſenſes, for the exiſtence of ſuch objects, as are removed by *diſtance* out of the ſphere of their operation. This teſtimony of ſenſe can continue no longer, than while the ſenſes continue to act. Their teſtimony does, and muſt *ceaſe* with their action. What therefore we are not *ſure* of by the *preſent*, i. e. the exiſting teſtimony of our ſenſes, *may* possibly be false, but what *may* possibly be false, cannot *necessarily* be true, that is, cannot be *certain*. And therefore, whatever becomes of the plain judgment of *common sense*, we must doubt of the existence of all such parts of the material world as are not the present objects of our senses. For, with respect to knowledge, there are only two states of mind, certainty and doubt; and of course where the former does not obtain, the latter must. But the works of creation, or the effects of these works upon each other furnish all the objects of that sort of knowledge which we receive through the senses; and therefore this knowledge is a standing and continual proof of the existence of God; which does and must attend the (constant) action of our senses.

Mr. Kett instances, in Berkely and Hume, as some of those visionary writers whose fanciful systems rose from pursuing Locke's principles. It would have been much more to his purpose had he shewn *what* these principles were, and *how* they led to such systems. With the same attention to *precise* proof he quotes Warburton's works *at large;* surely in such a voluminous writer he should not only have quoted the *particular* words, but also have referred to the particular place where they are to be found. Or is it that he thought with his fellow academic, Dr. Knox, to establish truth by the argument of *authority*, just as another of his fellow academics thought to establish it by the argument of *etymology*.

Mr. Kett tells us, that Mr. Locke contributed more than any other writer to the knowledge of thofe powers of the human mind, by which mankind are peculiarly diftinguifhed. What then is this new faculty which Mr. Kett introduces to us under the title of *common fenfe ;* a faculty which it feems prevents, or removes doubts, that cannot be difpelled by all thofe wonderful faculties with which Mr. Locke brings us acquainted? What is the object of its action, or the mode of its operation? And wherein does it differ from thofe other powers of the mind which Mr. Locke fo clearly explains? Till Mr. Kett is pleafed to give us fome more precife account of it, than he has yet done, we muft beg to be excufed from confidering it as worthy of attention. Or is Mr. Kett giving us a fample of it, when at p. 14. Vol. iii. of his firft edit. or p. 129. Vol. ii. of his fecond edit. he accufes certain proteftant writers of quitting the *ftrong holds* of Scripture doctrine, and arguing upon what *they* called, the *principles* of *natural* religion. It fhould feem however, as if neither thefe proteftant writers, nor their corrector, knew much of either the one, or the other. An attention to what is meant by the ftrong holds of Scripture doctrine, and what by natural religion, would have fhewn him that the charge was abfurd, becaufe the crime was impoffible. For what do we mean by natural religion, but the knowledge of *fuch* truths refpecting God, as can be collected by human reafon, from a confideration of his works? And is it poffible

that such truths should at all clash with those
truths, which he is pleased to *declare*, that is with
the doctrines of revelation ? And what were these
principles of natural religion for which Mr. Kett's
proteftant writers fo injudicioufly forfook the ftrong
holds of Scripture doctrine ? Why the admiffion
" that faith depends not upon the will, but upon
the underftanding," that " when the evidence for
the truth of a propofition is *full* and *clear*, this evidence *conftrains* affent, but that no blame is im-
putable for rejecting a propofition for which the
mind cannot fee evidence ; and that we are *not*
called upon to *believe*, what we *cannot* comprehend." Who thefe proteftant writers were, who
could not fee the difference between the principles
of logic, and thofe of natural religion I know not ;
but to whatever fpecies of knowledge thefe principles may belong, they certainly belong no more to
natural religion, than they do to natural philofophy. If by *faith* you mean the *mere fimple* act of
the underftanding, expreffed by the word belief ;
(abftracted from all confideration of the influence,
which the fubject matter of fuch belief *ought* to
have upon the conduct,) the *naked* affent of the
mind to the truth of a propofition, not admitting
demonftration, or fenfible proof : if by the *full* and
clear evidence for the truth of a propofition, you
mean demonftration, and if you further mean that
men are not blameable for withholding their affent
to propofitions, of which no *fufficient* proof is
given : and of *this* fufficiency they *themfelves* muft

judge at their *own* peril (for it is *this* circum-
ſtance which conſtitutes a ſtate of trial) nothing
certainly can be more true, than theſe aſſertions.
And had Mr. Kett's views of *revealed* religion been
a whit clearer than thoſe which he ſeems to have of
natural, or had his knowledge of the powers of the
human mind, and their reſpective operations, been
as diſtinct, as thoſe perſons ought to have, who
take upon them to criticiſe Mr. Locke, he would
have better underſtood the nature of what he calls
the ſtrong holds of Scripture doctrine, and what
the difference of the ideas is which reſpect the very
diſtinct operations of the mind from which knowledge and belief ariſe. But we will not follow the
example of Mr. Kett, in bringing *general* and *un-*
ſupported charges.

One great purpoſe of revelation is, to bring men
acquainted with *ſuch* truths, as they are *unable* to
diſcover by the *cuſtomary* uſe of their *natural* faculties, or with *ſuch* facts as their *cuſtomary* experience might incline them to disbelieve. Not as
Mr. Kett affirms to give them information which
they cannot underſtand ; yet ſuch muſt be the caſe
if men can be called upon, i. e. be under *moral*
obligations to *believe* what they *cannot comprehend*.
The whole knowledge of revelation is a knowledge
of *facts*, or of the conſequences of *theſe* facts.
This knowledge is *now* conveyed to mankind only
through the medium of human language. Can we
then believe the truth of theſe facts, or the reality
of theſe effects without comprehending the mean-

ing of the words by which thefe truths are conveyed to us? If you fay we *can*, then all tranflations of the Scriptures are *needlefs* : for wherefore are they tranflated, but becaufe men do not underftand the original tongues, that is, becaufe otherwife, men would not be able to comprehend what they are called upon to believe.

Human knowledge is received by feveral different ways, and this knowledge is called by different names, according to the different ways by which it is received ; but in whatever way it is received, unlefs the ideas of which it is compofed are clear and diftinct, it ceafes to be knowledge, we can learn nothing from fuch imperfect information. It is juft the fame as if the faculties of the mind were *unable* to perceive, or thofe of the body were incapable of tranfmitting the impreffions of external cbjects; or as if we were *ignorant* of the ideas ufually annexed to the words which we hear or fee.---
But further——

The only circumftance in which thefe various forts of knowledge differ from each other, is in the degree of probability naturally attendant upon each fort. That knowledge therefore which arifes from our *own* perceptions, and that which we receive from the information of other beings vary only in their probability, which may approach nearer to abfolute certainty than by any affigned difference. And the *degree* of probability, attached to each fort of knowledge, depends, not upon the clearnefs or obfcurity of the ideas compofing fuch knowledge, but upon the manner by which it is received. A lie is not lefs a lie for being more or lefs clearly underftood. Now certain knowledge arifes from our perceptions *only*, whether *internal* or *external*; it wholly depends upon the *accuracy* of our *natural* powers; but probable knowledge (which arifes chiefly from the information of others, and is the peculiar fubject of faith, built upon mere human teftimony) depends not upon the ftrength of our original powers, i. e. of thofe powers which our Creator has given us, fo much as upon our acquired dexterity in the ufe of them : and judgment is that operation of the mind by which we eftimate the *value* of probability. For judgment is not a faculty of the mind, but, like attention and confideration, an act of the underftanding. The perceptive faculties then, i. e. our original powers, enable us to *difcern* the various circumftances upon which the probability of events depends, and by the judgment we are enabled to eftimate the value of this probability. But we can no more eftimate the value of probability, than we can difcern the circumftances upon which it depends, unlefs the ideas relating to both thefe matters, are *clear* and diftinct, that is, unlefs we comprehend them. It is impoffible therefore to exercife any act of faith about matters of which we are intirely ignorant : *fome* knowledge we muft have; but though this knowledge may be more, or lefs particular, yet it muft be clear, and we cannot believe any farther than it is fo; that is, we can *no more* believe, than *we can* know what we do *not*

comprehend. An inftance will explain this matter. All perfons, who are convinced of the truth
of the Scriptures; muft believe that Jefus is the
Son of God ; yet no perfon believes that Jefus is
the Son of God in the *fame way* that he believes,
every man-child born into the world, is the fon of
his father. This *no* perfon believes, becaufe *every*
perfon *knows* it to be impoffible, in the literal fenfe
of the words, according to all human acceptation.
But we believe not what we *cannot* comprehend,
but what we perfectly can : that as children derive
their exiftence, not from any act of their own, but
from their parents, fo Chrift derived his exiftence
from God, John v. 26. Thus faith is ιλιγχος πραγμάτων
μ' Ελερομίνων---the proof of *matters* which are *not* objects of fenfe to us, and which therefore admit of
no other proof than teftimony. But teftimony
which we can not underftand, that is, information
which we cannot comprehend, is no information at
all. 1 Cor. xiv. 11.
Such however is the force of prejudice, aided by
confufed and imperfect knowledge, that many good
perfons are perfuaded, that both themfelves, and
others *believe*, what they *cannot* comprehend. Yet
is there juft as much difference between believing
the truth, i. e. the reality of a matter of fact, and
believing the *way* by which fuch matter of fact has
been brought to pafs, as there is between experi-
encing our *own belief* of a matter of fact, and experi-
encing the *fact* itfelf. When therefore our belief
of the creation is urged as an inftance of our believ-

ing what we do not comprehend, becaufe we do not comprehend *how*, or by *what particular* means, God made the world, the argument has no force. Becaufe though all perfons believe that God made the world, no perfons believe *how*, or by what particular means, he made it. But it is *that* matter *only* which we do not comprehend. We know the world exifts by the teftimony of our fenfes ; and we know from reafon that things cannot create themfelves, that being to act, *before* they had the power of acting. He therefore who built all things is God.

Juft in the fame way as thefe good people cannot fee the difference between believing the exiftence of a matter of fact, and believing the way *by which* this exiftence is produced ; fo neither can they fee the difference between the information communicated by pofitive, or by (what are called) negative ideas. (See Hey's Norrifian Lectures, Vol. III. Book IV. Introduction to Part II. Sect. vii. p. 124.) Yet from this latter fort of information we do not learn what a thing *is*, but what it *is not*. A very fcanty fpecies of knowledge indeed ! But upon the ground of this imaginary knowledge it has been faid, " you believe that God is a fpirit, that is, you believe what you cannot comprehend. To be fure no perfon comprehends what a fpirit is, the term fpirit conveys only a negative idea. A fpirit hath *not* flefh and bones. But though you do not comprehend what a fpirit

C

is, neither do you *believe* what a fpirit is : you only
believe what it is *not ;* it is not any fuch matter
as you are acquainted with ; and this you. *fully*
comprehend. You believe God does not confift of
any fuch matter as you are acquainted with. Can
any thing be more intelligible ?

But it is not merely a want of *clear* ideas, and
precife knowledge, a common, but utterly groundlefs prejudice, refpecting the nature of myfteries,
has contributed not a little to eftablifh this notion
of the poffibility of believing what we cannot comprehend ; i. e. what is unintelligible. It has been
imagined that myfteries, *as* myfteries, made a *ne-*
ceffary part of revealed religion ; as if it was *re-*
quifite, that revelation fhould never be *without* fome
parts unintelligible, and incomprehenfible to the
human underftanding. But though it is reafonable
to expect that we fhould be left ignorant of many
things both in the works, and the word of God ;
and though many important ends may be anfwered,
by things being kept fecret for *fome time*, yet what
benefit can poffibly arife from fecrets which are
never to be revealed ? It cannot therefore be of
the effence of a myftery that it fhould *never* be dif-
clofed : for that is to make it effential to a myftery
that it fhould be *ufelefs.* And we may obferve,
that *this* word is moft ufually applied in Scripture
to matters which *once* were fecrets, but which for
certain important reafons are *now* revealed, Matt.
xiii. 11. Rom. xi. 25. xvi. 25. Eph. iii. 4.*

---

* A fondnefs for the delufive moon-fhine of imagination, and an
averfion to the *clear* and *ftrong* light of reafon, fo confpicuous in many

A want of ability to perceive the difference, between *original* and *tranfmitted* revelation, and the
metaphorical expreffion, the *word* of *God*, affect-
edly applied to the Scriptures,* has occafioned
many perfons to afcribe the fame authority to the
writings of infpired men, as is due to the *immediate*, and if I may fo fay, *perfonal* declarations of
God himfelf; and it has been asked refpecting the
prefent affurance of faith, " what then, does not
the evidence of God carry *certainty* along with it ?
Undoubtedly it does. God has unqueftionably
given information to particular perfons, at fundry
times, and in divers manners ; in dreams, and vi-
fions, and by an audible voice, as well as by the

---

pious perfons, leads them equally afide from the truth in contrary directions. Thus while fome are fo eager to make myfteries a neceffary
part of revelation, others write as if they meant to difcard every
thing of that kind from *it ;* and fo the author of the Horæ Solitariæ de-
duces almoft all the peculiarities of Chriftianity from the verbal expreffions of the *Jewifh* Scriptures; infomuch that the antient Jews (if
they underftood their own mother tongue as well as this author) muft
have been very little behind the Apoftles (even after the defcent of
the Holy Ghoft) in their knowledge of Chriftian falvation. And though
Paul profited in the knowledge of the Mofaic economy above many
of his own countrymen, and though he received his knowledge of the
Chriftian difpenfation from the author of it, Gal. i. 12. yet muft he
have been ftrangely miftaken when he afferts that what he fpoke was
the *hidden* wifdom of God, which in other ages was *not* made *known*
to (any of) the fons of men; if it be true (as this author afferts) that
our prefent very imperfect knowledge of the Hebrew tongue is fufficient to prove the very contrary.

* All that any man (fays Dr. Hey, Norrifian Lectures, B. I.
Chap. i. Sect. 6. & Chap. xii. Sect. 14. parag. 2. in vol. I. pages 4, &
111. & B. IV. Introduction to Part 2d. Sect. 14. p. 131) fhould
really be underftood to mean, when he fpeaks of the word of God,
is human interpretations of it.

incomprehenfible mode of fecret infpiration. But in all thefe cafes, they who received fuch information, received, we may be fure, unqueftionable *marks* of the divinity of it, though we are, and muft be ignorant of the nature of *thefe* marks. For had not this been the cafe, every idle fancy of folly, and every extravagant freak of enthufiafm might have paffed for divine revelation. At prefent however we know of no other mark by which we can be affured that we receive truth upon the *immediate* evidence of God, but that it has been miraculoufly conveyed to us. We may indeed reafonably prefume that words fpoken to us by God himfelf, muft be free from all uncertainty, becaufe God not only clearly knows what Himfelf means ; He alfo knows *as* clearly, whether his communication is *perfeEtly* underftood ; but this cannot be the cafe with knowledge communicated by any other being, fince God *alone* knoweth the thoughts. But when original revelation is tranfmitted to us by uninfpired men (and in thefe days we have no other) by the *ufual* mode of human communication, i. e. by human language, fuch information muft (without a miracle) partake of all the imperfeEtions, and uncertainty, of this imperfeEt, and uncertain mode of communication.

Mr. Kett thinks himfelf juftified, if *not* in the *truth* at leaft in the *propriety* of bringing thefe charges againft Mr. Locke, by the authority of Warburton and Mackintofh, who Mr. Kett affirms, (p. 17. Vol. iii. edit. i. or p. 131. Vol. ii. edit. ii.) juftly

obferve, " that we cannot exceed the bounds prefcribed for human knowledge, without involving
ourfelves in contradiction and abfurdity : that
nothing has produced more pernicious mifchief to
fociety, than the purfuit of principles in themfelves good, far beyond the bounds, in which they
are good." Now what are we to underftand in
this place by principles ? Not principles of *mere*
knowledge furely ! Thefe may be *true*, or *falfe*;
but whoever thought of intuitive truths, which is
what we ufually mean by principles being *good*
or *bad* ? Not principles of morality ! For thefe,
if good, muft for *ever* continue to be good. There
are no bounds, or limits to what is fit, right, proper, commendable, praife-worthy in *itfelf*, after
which it becomes unfit, wrong, improper, wicked,
deteftable, abominable. When we defcribe moral
principles as *right* in *themfelves*, we mean that
they are *eternally* right, that they do not admit of
any change. That truth, juftice, humanity, honefty, cannot become falfehood, fraud, cruelty,
knavery, how far foever carried. Or are we to
fuppofe that thefe authors meant, what *alone can*
be meant, principles of *expediency* or *utility*; all
this may be very true, but is very trifling. Becaufe who fees not that the general benefit of mankind muft depend upon a great variety of circumftances, for which no *fixed* rule can poffibly be
given ?

But what are *thefe bounds* prefcribed for human
knowledge ? and who has prefcribed them ? The

powers of the human mind are certainly not unlimited, but who can fay what thefe limits are? Ideas fuggefted by external objects, and thefe ideas varioufly modified by the different faculties of the underftanding, are the materials of all our knowledge; and where ideas are either abfolutely wanting, or are much confufed, and very obfcure, we fhall either have no knowledge at all, or it will be exceedingly imperfect; which of thefe two is the cafe with Meffrs. Milner and Kett, the public muft determine; and thofe who can find out Mr. Locke's faults by the light fuch writers afford, muft have good eyes indeed.

Mr. Kett has alfo recourfe to teftimony for the proof of the mifchiefs generated by Mr. Locke's miftakes; and when he *produces* this teftimony, or thofe miftakes upon which this teftimony is founded, it will be time enough to confider of a reply to fuch vague, *confufed* and unmeaning, accufations.

Dr. Napleton, in his advice to ftudents in divinity, follows not a little the practice of Meffrs. Milner and Kett; and at p. 34, warns thofe who read Mr. Locke's Theological writings, " to be cautious how they follow his opinions in fuch paffages of Scripture as relate to the divinity of our Lord, or the affiftance of the Holy Spirit." He would have done more credit to the *fairnefs* of his advice, if he had pointed out the exceptionable paffages, and to the *value* of it, if he had pointed

out his reasons for thinking these passages exceptionable.

Bishop Horne also has thought proper to contro-
vert Mr. Locke's notions of civil government ;
but he has done it, as all honest inquirers after
truth ought to do, by endeavouring to shew the
falsity of Mr. Locke's reasoning ; with what suc-
cess the readers of this defence of Mr. Locke, must
determine.

The Bishop begins his Discourse upon the Origin
of civil government, with observing, " that
it is a natural, and a laudable curiosity to inquire
into the origin of civil government, and to know
at *what* time, and under *whose* direction, an insti-
tution was devised capable of contributing so much
to the production, furtherance, and establishment
of human happiness." It would be a curiosity
equally natural, and equally laudable, to inquire
into, and ascertain, at *what* time, and under whose
direction, the various arts of life, which contribute
so much to the comfort and well being of mankind were *invented*, and by *whom* they were brought
to their present state of perfection. And is not
each of these inquiries equally practicable ? And
does not the nature and constitution of this world
plainly shew, that both are alike impossible ? Not
only the *constitution* of that *nature*, which God has
unalterably appointed, is a progressive one; that
state of happiness also, which mankind are enabled
to attain, by the exertion of those faculties which
God has given them, is likewise a progressive state.

The productions of nature can no more reach that degree of perfection they are capable of at *once*, or of a sudden, than the habits and difpositions of the moral, the wifdom of the intellectual, or the dexterity and addrefs of the active world. Time and labour, and cultivation, muft mature the firft ; attention, diligence, and repeated efforts muft complete the laft. Whatever the ftate of our firft parents, of the animal, vegetable, and material world might be, it was, and muft be totally different, from that of each individual thing, which was to fucceed. The *origin* of a ftate of nature, and the *continuance* of *that* ftate, have nothing in common. The firft was a miracle, not to be repeated ; the fecond, though no lefs wonderful, lofes the name of miracle, from its continual repetition. We know no more how the natural and moral world were fet agoing, than we know how the planets were projected in their orbits, and you might juft as well ask when an acorn became an oak, a child a man, or when London became a city, as to ask at *what* time, and under whofe direction civil government was eftablifhed ? The Britifh government is univerfally and defervedly admired ; but who can fay *when*, and under whofe direction it was, or whether it is even *yet* eftablifhed ? It has received gradual improvements and amendments, through a long courfe of year's, and will probably continue to do fo pro re nata. Its various excellencies were attained by flow degrees, and are no more the worfe for being the fruit of ſtrife and contention, than the religion of Chriſt is, Philip. i. 15. and provided the happineſs of mankind is but promoted, we have unqueſtionable cauſe to rejoice, and as lovers of our country may ſay with the Apoſtle, "yea and we will rejoice." To take an inſtance in our own memory. During the long adminiſtration of Sir Robert Walpole, whenever the miniſter was teaſed with a troubleſome pamphlet, he uſed to ſend his myrmidons with a *general* warrant to ſearch the printing-offices for treaſonable papers ; not indeed with the hopes, or even the expectations of finding any, but merely to plague the *oppoſition* printers, by overturning their *caſes* and making *pye* of their *letter;* becauſe he had nothing upon which he could ground a legal proceſs. But theſe *general* warrants have ſince been declared *illegal*, and now no miniſter dares to iſſue them, and we may venture to predict never will. The Biſhop indeed ſpeaks of civil ſociety as if it was the invention of an hour, or the work of a day. For, who that thought otherwiſe, would expect to aſcertain " at *what* time, and under whoſe direction, a machine was conſtructed capable, by a variety of well adjuſted ſprings and movements, of controlling the irregularities of depraved nature, &c. and ſecuring to us the numerous benefits of government."

Ariſtocratic and democratic forms of government, the Biſhop tells us are *illegitimate* forms of government.—No law ſurely but that of God can ordain a form of government for *all* mankind. These friends of the good Bishop then, who thought his Sermon worth republishing in that wise compilation, called the Scholar Armed, would be kind to his memory and his reputation, if they would tell us in what part of the Bible these forms are declared to be illegitimate ; and also in what part of it a description of that legitimate form is to be found, which the Bishop and his friends seem so anxious to establish. Whether his, and their anxiety arose from a desire to derive every thing from a religious original, just as certain other pious persons were anxious to derive all arts and sciences, from the Bible, I know not; but considering how very careful good persons often are of their own interest, it would not be strange, if having heard of that celebrated maxim, " no bishop, no king," they might be apprehensive, the converse should be no less true. However when these friends of his Lordship can shew where directions for this legitimate form of government are to be found in the word of God, I will undertake to answer those questions which the Bishop asks with such an air of triumph, viz. *Where* the universal assembly was convened ? and who had authority to convene it ? and how the proceedings of this assembly were regulated, &c. &c.?*

* Had the Bishop's understanding been as good as his dispositions he would have seen, that when writers on *moral* subjects (meaning by moral subjects, such subjects as respect the conduct of mankind) describe the manner in which such conduct may be attained : they do not mean to describe the conduct which *actually*, and in fact prevails, but such as would prevail, were men governed by their reason,

To fathers in their private families, fays the Biſhop, after Mr. Hooker (whom by the by with the uſual honeſty of polemical writers, he can either quote, or paſs over in ſilence, as beſt ſuits his purpoſe) nature has given ſupreme power.

judging, from the nature, and faculties their Creator has given them, and the ſituation and circumſtances in which he has placed them. Juſt as mathematicians, when they demonſtrate the various properties of different figures, mean only to ſhew the *relations* between certain *ideas*. For theſe relations no longer obtain when you paſs from *abſtract* ideas to *real* exiſtence. Not a ſingle propoſition in Euclid is true of a triangle drawn upon paper, or cut out of any material whatſoever ; that is, when from ideas in the mind they become objects of our corporeal ſenſes. It is unqueſtionably true that the three angles of a triangle are *exactly* equal to two right ones. But draw the figure, and the propoſition, as referred to *that* figure, or to any triangular figure, in which matter is concerned, is no longer true. Thus again we are told, that " by the firſt law of motion, a body when acted upon by a ſingle impulſe, will continue to move uniformly *for ever*, and will *for ever* perſevere in its *original* direction. Yet when this law is applied to matter *actually* exiſting, it *ceaſes* to be true. Nobody ever ſaw *ſuch* motion. So again, when Sir Iſaac Newton diſcovered that the moon's motion was of the *like* kind, that it would be, if the *law* of gravitation, obſervable upon the *ſurface* of the *earth*, reached to that planet ; he did not mean to aſſert, that gravitation was the *cauſe* of the moon's motion ; becauſe for aught any one can tell, an angel may carry it about, but he meant to ſhew that ſuch a force would produce the *ſame* effect. And when writers aſſert certain matters relative to civil government, or church authority, they do not mean to aſſert, that civil government, or church authority, *actually* aroſe from ſuch circumſtances, but that theſe circumſtances would certainly produce *ſuch* civil government and ſuch church authority, as in the want of either, would anſwer the ends *propoſed* by ſuch inſtitutions.

Proofs that matters *can* ariſe from certain circumſtances may be derived from abſtract reaſoning, proofs, that matters *actually did* ariſe from certain circumſtances, can only be derived from our *own* experience, or from *that* of others, made known to us by their teſtimony. Thoſe therefore who aſſert that the writers upon civil ſociety have contributed to the madneſs of French philoſophy, miſunderſtand the nature of the reaſoning employed by theſe writers.

Nature ! The God of nature furely ! The term nature is a *mere* word, and when we talk of the gifts of nature, we mean thofe gifts of God, thofe powers, faculties, qualifications, qualities, which he beftows *indifcriminately*, though perhaps not equally upon all the various fpecies of beings refpectively : and from confidering thefe various natural powers, faculties, &c. we collect the purpofes they were intended to anfwer, and of courfe the end for which they were given : and this is the *great* and *general* argument of final caufes from which moft of our knowledge is derived. What then, I afk, are the purpofes for which this fupreme power is given ? and why is it given by *nature* to fathers *only*, and not to mothers ? and how does it appear that this power is given to *one* parent *only* ? and what are we to underftand by *fupreme power* ? If I have any ideas to the words fupreme power, it means the higheft poffible degree of power, which can be exercifed over whatever is the object of it. Now the higheft degree of power which human creatures can exercife over living beings is, the power of life and death. What then are thofe circumftances of mankind, from which we are to conclude, that *nature* gives *this fupreme* power, i. e. the power of *life* and *death* over their offspring to fathers in their private families ? what is the ufe of fuch a power, and why is it given to the father only, and not to the mother ? of whom the Bifhop fays nothing !

Or is it meant only to fhew that *fome fort* of

power does, and muſt exiſt amongſt mankind ?
But whatever power may exiſt amongſt men, natural reaſon, and divine revelation equally ſhew
that it cannot be the *right* (for that is what we
mean in the preſent caſe by the word power) of
life and death, except in the caſe of ſelf-defence.
In civil ſociety indeed men may agree to eſtabliſh
any puniſhment for offences againſt the *State* (ſuch
are all crimes in the proper ſenſe of the word)
which they may think proper. Becauſe all puniſhments for *crimes* are upon the ground of *ſelf-defence*, nor can ſuch an agreement be unjuſt. *Public* puniſhments when not inflicted upon the innocent, may be *harſh*, or *cruel*, but they cannot be
unjuſt. But what is all this to the eſtabliſhment
of civil power ? a power inſtituted for very different purpoſes, than thoſe of fathers in their private
families. Political and paternal power differ ſo
much in the *ends* to be anſwered by them, that no
inference can be made, nor any concluſion drawn
from one to the other. A father may bring up his
children in what religion he pleaſes ; and he has this
power (right) if he has it any way by *nature*.
But may a king provide ſuch religion for his ſubjects as he thinks proper, and *compel* them to receive it ? Indeed nothing but the utmoſt ignorance of human nature, and the ſtrongeſt prejudice could make any perſon entertain a notion that
civil government, can have any *other end* than the
temporal benefit of mankind ; or any other foundation, than the *actual* or *tacit* conſent, (whatever

the motives to fuch confent may be) of thofe,
who for their *general* intereft, fubmit to it.

What work men made, when the fafhion was to
determine the *origin* and *form* of civil government,
the extent of authority, and the degree of fubjec-
tion due to it, (not from the reafons of things, the
laws of our common nature, the practice of particular nations, the tempers, character, and difpofitions of mankind in different ages and countries
but) from precepts, and precedents, fuppofed to
be contained in the Bible, will, one fhould think,
never be forgotten in *this* nation. And what could
follow from fo injudicious an appeal to, and fo abfurd an application of holy fcripture, than what
did follow, confufion and ftrife, and every evil
work ? For while *one* party efteemed monarchy
the appointment of God, and princes the Lord's
anointed, the other concluded from the *fame* authority, and therefore with *equal* reafon, that
kings were given by God in his anger to fcourge
the folly of the people who defired them. But an
impartial reader of the fcriptures muft have *clearly*
perceived, how little ground there is in them for
fuch decifions : becaufe we no where find any thing
more than *general* exhortations to fubmit to government, to honour magiftrates, to be obedient
to laws : all thefe matters are the duties of fub-
jects---not a word of the duties of governors ; and
have they therefore no duties ? Nor is the leaft
hint given in the word of God, that any particular
form is either more *preferable* to others, or more

acceptable to him. We no where find any defcrip-
tions of the feveral orders of magiftrates; any no-
tices of the particular powers with which they
fhould be invefted; any declarations by whofe confent or authority the laws fhould be eftablifhed,
or annulled, altered, or executed. And what is of
no lefs importance, (though very feldom attended
to) viz. that had the form of civil government
been thus *exprefsly* appointed of Grd, it muft either
have admitted of *no defects*, or *no remedies* for them.
The conftitution of the Englifh government is defervedly efteemed the moft excellent in the world;
but could this judicious Bifhop, or can his equally
judicious admirers find a limited monarchy in the
Bible ? This conftitution has arrived at this high
degree of excellence by *numerous*, *flow*, and *repeated*
alterations, all which, were monarchy, the appointment of God, would, *without* the *fame* appointment, have been utterly finful.——So much for the
political abilities of thofe zealous perfons who
thought fit to countenance this courtly publication
of the Scholar Armed: their republication of
Mr. Willat's Sermon againft the Religion of Nature, is an equal proof of their knowledge, and
difcernment.

OBSERVATIONS, &c.

IT is one thing to enquire into the nature of the *effects* produced by our mental powers, or into the confequences of the operations of our intellectual faculties, and quite another matter to enquire, *how* thefe powers act, or by *what means* thefe effects are produced. Mr. Locke, therefore, with a fagacity fimilar to that of another great genius, Sir Ifaac Newton, "wifely declined, B. I. Chap. i. Sect. 2. medling with the phyfical confideration of the mind, or troubling himfelf to examine wherein its *effence* confifts, or by what *motions* of the *fpirits*, or *alterations* of our *bodies*, we come to have any fenfation by our organs, or any ideas in our underftandings, and whether thofe ideas do, in their formation, any, or all of them, depend on matter, &c." Yet he fays, B. II. Chap. viii. Sect. 4. "that were he *inclined* to *enquire* into the *natural caufes*, and *manner* of *perception*, he fhould endeavour to fhew how fenfation, that is, ideas may be produced in us by external objects; viz. by *different degrees* and *modes* of *motion* in our *animal fpirits*, varioufly agitated by thefe external objects." This motion he fuppofes, Sect. 12. muft be continued from thefe objects to the brain, *there* to produce in our minds the different ideas of fuch objects. And he goes on, Ibid. "but fince bodies of an *obfervable* bignefs *can* be perceived (by the fenfes) at a diftance," (that is, fince bodies that can be perceived—*can* be perceived) "and

A

since *no* such bodies are ever perceived to pass from these objects to the brain; therefore," says Mr. Locke, it is *evident* that these bodies, which come from external objects to the brain, are—*imperceptible:*" and so it seems we have the evidence of *sense* for what is imperceptible—that is for what such evidence cannot possibly be had. But in Chap. xiv. Sect. 13. of this second Book he says, " that *not* knowing how the ideas of our minds are *framed*, of what *materials* they are *made*, whence they have their *light*, and *how* they come to make their appearance, he can give *no other* reason for these phænomena than that in *fact* they are so, see B. IV. Ch. iii. f. 11, 12, 13, 14. also Chap. vi. & x. f. 19. and this seems to be about as far as the human understanding can penetrate into this subject.

Whether Dr. Reid of Glasgow was disgusted with this unintelligible philosophy (as it is sometimes called) I know not, but he professes to make his inquiry into the human mind upon the principles of *common sense*; yet what he understands by common sense, or what he wishes his readers to understand by this word he does not inform us. He tells us indeed, Ch. i. f. 1. and with great truth, " that there is but *one* way to the knowledge of nature's works, the way of *observation* and *experiment*; and this great discovery, owing to the sagacity of a most *uncommon* genius, is one of Dr. Reid's maxims of *common sense:* yet at the beginning of his second section he assures us, " that to attend accurately to the operations of our own minds, and to make them an object of thought, is *no easy* matter to the *contemplative*; and to the *bulk* of *mankind* is next to impossible." And so it seems *this common* sense is very uncommon.

Common sense indeed can only consist of the *common* observations of *common* men, that is, of the bulk of mankind; collected it may be *without much*, perhaps

without *any* confideration and reflexion : and by philofophical knowledge can only be meant fuch knowledge (however lightly the Doctor may deem of it) as
is alone attained by much attention, confideration, and
reflexion. For confideration and reflexion can obtain
only in confequence of habits of thinking ; and a want
of common fenfe does not imply lunacy, as the Doctor
feems to think, but a *weaknefs* of the *perceptive* and
difcriminating powers.

Thofe then who know the advantages of clear
notions and diftinct knowledge ; and thofe who know
how much attention, confideration, and reflexion contribute to clear notions, and diftinct knowledge, will
alfo know how to appreciate the refpective values
of philofophical and common fenfe.

Had the Doctor propofed to make his inquiry into
the (nature and powers of the) human mind upon the
principles of *common fenfation*, (or as Mr. Locke fpeaks,
B. I. Chap. i. f. 2. by confidering the difcerning faculties of a man, as they are *employed* about the objects
they have to do with) comprehending under this expreffion of common fenfation, the *whole* of our perceptions, both *internal* and *external*, he would certainly
have been nearer the mark, but then he would not
have appeared to have been any wifer than Mr. Locke,
a matter he feems not a little defirous of.

Mr. Profeffor Dugald Stewart in his Outlines of
Moral Philofophy fays nothing of the principles upon
which he makes his inquiry, into the nature and powers
of the human mind, but he begins very judicioufly
with confidering *that faculty* by which we receive information of the operations of its feveral *powers*, from the
exercife of *which we can* alone collect its nature. This
information we can receive *only* through our own confcioufnefs, and can communicate to other men *only* by
the ufe of *language*. Now this *internal* experience of

what paffes in our own mind, differs intirely from that experience which we receive through our *fenfes* of what paffes in the world about us; namely, from the experience fuggefted to us by the action, or as it is fometimes called, by the impreffion of external objects upon our corporeal fenfes. For the *reality* of our experience which relates to the effects of external objects upon our bodily fenfes, can be afcertained to *other* men by fubjecting thefe *fame* objects to *their* fenfes. But we have *no way* of afcertaining the reality of our own confcioufnefs, that is, the reality of our own internal perceptions, by which we can prove, that what we allege is not *mere imagination*. Thus, the apoftles and prophets were *confcious* of the truth conveyed to their minds by divine infpiration, and they were confcious that the truth *fo* conveyed to them, was conveyed by God Himfelf: but when it was neceffary to afcertain to *other* men this infpiration, that is, the *reality* of this *alledged* confcioufnefs, they were empowered to work miracles in atteftation of their allegation.

Confcioufnefs is an infeparable concomitant of all operations of every mental faculty as Mr. Stewart obferves, at the *time* of fuch *operation*; but what Mr. S. does not obferve, this confcioufnefs is often continued to the individual through life. Yet is confcioufnefs as different from memory, as memory is different from imagination, although Doctor Reid confounds them together, fee Chap. i. f. 2. and affirms that they are the *fame*. We find a fimilar confufion of ideas in Mr. Stewart's Philofophy of the human mind, in page 133. 8vo. Chap. iii. who in the fame manner confounds memory, and what he calls conception together. He there tells us " that by conception he means *that* power of the mind which enables us to form a notion of an *abfent* object of perception, or of fenfation. I do not contend he fays that this is *exclufively* the proper meaning of the word, but I think the faculty which I have now defined (defcribed he fhould have faid, had he known the difference between a *definition* and a *defcription*) deferves to be diftinguifhed by an appropriated name." To be fure if we mean to difcourfe intelligibly upon the powers of the human mind, every diftinct faculty muft have an *appropriated* name. Mr. S. goes on "conception is often confounded with other powers. When a painter makes a picture of a friend who is abfent or dead, he is *commonly* faid to paint from *memory*, and the expreffion is fufficiently correct for *common converfation*." Every body I believe but this Profeffor would think it fufficiently correct for *philofophical accuracy*. "But fays Mr. S. in the analyfis of the mind there is ground for diftinction. Certainly there is and therefore I diftinguifh between memory and conception, as well as between memory and confcioufnefs." The power of conception enables the painter," Mr. S. tells us, "to make the features of his friend an object of thought, fo as to copy the refemblance," and he adds the power of *memory* recognifes the features as a former object of perception," the power of memory both in the painter and in all who knew the countenance of the perfon pourtrayed. Mr. S. goes on "every act of memory includes an idea of the paft. Conception implies *no* idea of time," no more does the exercife of many other faculties of the human mind. Now comes the conclufion "Thus the word (the *act* the profeffor means of) conception correfponds to what the fchoolmen call, *fimple apprehenfion*. Strange that a learned profeffor fhould thus bewilder himfelf. A little clofe attention and clear reflexion would have fhewn him that the mind has a power of recalling fuch ideas as have *once* been the object of its thoughts; and as no idea is ever prefented to the mind *fingle* and *alone*, it can feparate *thefe collections* of ideas, which have thus been prefented by external objects

together, or, in company with each other, and can
confider *any one*, without attending to any other: thus
it can confider the idea of whitenels, whether it be prefented to the fight from a fwan, from fnow, from milk,
or from any other object. And as the mind can feparate
the various ideas received in *company*, it can alfo make
arbitrary combinations of thefe ideas at pleafure, according to the Poet

> Humano capiti cervicem pictor equinam
> Jungere fi velit, et varias inducere plumas.
> *Undique collatis membris*, ut turpiter atrum
> Definat in pifcem, mulier formofa fuperne.

And wherefore is this picture introduced ? not to fhew
the abfurdity of memory, which *cannot* be abfurd, but
to fhew the abfurdity of conception, that is, of imagination which *can*. Again, conceive, fays a mathematician, a curve line,—conceive that it returns into
itfelf—conceive a point to be taken within the curve,
and conceive this point to be placed at an equal diftance from every part of the curve. By this arbitrary
combination of ideas, he forms a curve of a particular fort, that is, having particular relations, from
which arife properties peculiar to this curve; all
which he can deduce from this arbitrary combination
of ideas.

In like manner had Dr. Reid attended to the two
faculties of memory and confcioufnefs, he muft, one
fhould think, have feen the difference ; becaufe we are
confcious of the *prefent* acts of our own minds, but we
can only *remember* what is *paft*. Common fenfe, of
which he is fo fond, might have informed him, that
we *cannot* remember what is *prefent*.

The confufion of ideas indeed, which prevails in
both thefe Scottifh Profeffors, is truly wonderful. In
Chap. ii. f. 4. & 5, Dr. Reid confounds belief, know-

ledge, and judgment together. At page 30 he tells us, that fenfation and remembrance are natural principles of belief: at p. 34, 35, 37 he confiders belief and knowledge as the *fame* act of the mind. Yet no two acts of the mind can be more *different*, or more *diftinct* from each other. Whatever truth admits of *intuitive*, or *demonftrative*, or *fenfible* evidence, is *knowledge*; fuch truth is *certain:* whatever truth does *not* admit of one, or the other, of *thefe forts* of proof, is a matter of belief. Whatever is only believed, upon mere human teftimony, *may* be falfe, whatever is *known muft* be *true.* Knowledge produces *certainty*; belief only produces probability. The *affent* of the mind to knowledge is *unlimited* and *unalterable.* The affent of the mind to matters of belief is neither unlimited, nor unalterable. There may arife *reafons* for *retracting* our affent to the latter; it is impoffible that any reafons can arife for retracting our affent to the former. In the cafe of knowledge we *actually* perceive by the *ufe* of our *own* faculties, the relations between our ideas, in the cafe of belief, we rely upon the perceptions of other men, or rather upon the account they are pleafed to give us, of their perceptions.

With a like confufion in his ideas, Mr. Stewart talks of the *belief* with which *confcioufnefs* is attended. See Outlines, S. 1. Art. 9. He would not have talked in this manner if he had attended to the difference between knowledge and belief. The information received from *all* experience, whether it be the experience we have of the *ftate* of our own minds arifing from internal confcioufnefs; or the experience we have of the ftate of external objects arifing from *their* effect upon our corporeal fenfes, is attended with certainty: for if we cannot rely upon this information, the attainment of certain knowledge is impoffible: but belief is not attended with certainty. Belief therefore, and

knowledge cannot, as Mr. S. afferts, Outlines, S. 1.
Art. 9, reft upon the *same* foundation.—By judgment
we mean the power of *eftimating* the probability of any
matters propofed to our belief. It has nothing to do
with knowledge or certainty.

In page 212 of the Philofophy of the Human Mind,
edit. 8vo, 1802, Mr. S. fpeaks of the *inftinctive* principle, *directed* in its operation by the *experience* of the individual. If I underftand the fenfe of the word *inftinct*,
it means that *difpofition* in the animal world, which leads
the different forts of living creatures, not only to *purfue*
and *attain conftantly*, and *regularly certain ends*, but to
accomplifh this attainment, by a *fpecific*, and *uniform* mode
of doing it.

In Chap. ii. fect. 5. of Dr. Reid's Inquiry into the
Human Mind, the Doctor feems to apprehend that
much mifchief may arife from any endeavours to afcertain the meaning of the words we ufe. It is not a little
wonderful that a man who appears to have thought *fo
much*, fhould have confidered *fo little*, the only ufeful
purpofe of thinking; viz. that of attaining and communicating clear notions, and precife knowledge : and
that he fhould not have been able to fee, that it muft
be abfolutely impoffible to make any, the leaft advan-
ces in fcience, unlefs we affix clear and diftinct ideas
to the words we ufe. Yet he tells us, in the fection before us, that it is happy no man pretends to define fenfation and confcioufnefs; for that thofe who have defined, and explained belief, have contributed to the
production of the moft incredible paradoxes

At page 11. the Doctor tells us that Des Cartes inferred *his own* exiftence from the poffeffion of his power
of thinking; and the Doctor inquires from *what* that
philofopher inferred his poffeffion of the power of
thinking ? Was it the Doctor afks from confcioufnefs ?
and he further afks how a man can *know*, that his con-

fcioufnefs does not deceive him? and I afk how a man can *know* that his corporeal fenfes does not deceive him? becaufe unlefs we can rely upon our *internal* perceptions, and our *external* fenfations, for the *certainty* of their information, all knowledge is impoffible.

At page 26, the Doctor talks of that fenfe, whofe objects are *leaft* in danger of being miftaken for *other things*. What are we to underftand by thefe words "other things?" Is there any fenfe whofe objects are *leaft* in danger of being miftaken for the objects of other fenfes? The objects of every fenfe are as diftinct from each other, as the fenfes themfelves. A found is no more likely to be miftaken for bitternefs than the power of hearing for that of tafting: nor is there any more *fimplicity* in the fenfe of fmelling, or tafting, or hearing, than in that of fight. But perhaps the Doctor means, that the perceptions conveyed are more various in fome fenfes than others. Odours are only perceived by the fenfe of fmelling, founds only by that of hearing. But the touch fuppofe conveys the perception of heat, and cold, roughnefs and fmoothnefs, hardnefs and foftnefs, of ftraitnefs and curvature, of extenfion and folidity, and perhaps of figure, certainly of fome circumftances attending it, and it may be of fwiftnefs or flownefs of motion; and without doubt the moft various perceptions are thofe we receive through the fight. Different objects however affect different fenfes, and we are equally ignorant of the circumftances which render the different fenfes *fitted* to be *affected* by thefe different objects.

Natural philofophy, fays the Doctor, page 26, informs us, that all animal and vegetable bodies are continually fending forth *effluvia* of vaft *fubtilety*. Thefe volatile particles, the Doctor *thinks*, do probably repel each other, and fo fcatter themfelves in the air; and thus the fmell of plants and other bodies is caufed by thefe volatile

B

parts, &c. We know, by experiment, that air is the vehicle of found, but no experiment has yet been made to fhew that it is the vehicle of odours. And all this fine argument from what the Doctor calls natural philofophy, feems at beft but a groundlefs conjecture. This fubtile effluvia, and thefe volatile particles fly about in the air it feems, and we *know* they do fo, becaufe we fmell : and we fmell becaufe this fubtile effluvia,and thefe volatile particles fly about in the air. But the theory, to ufe the Doctor words, that all bodies are fmelled by means of effluvia, and volatile particles, which are drawn into the noftrils along with the air, is perhaps like many other theories, rather the product of the imagination, than of juft induction ; for the Doctor acknowledges, page 28, that the fenfation of fmelling, of itself could never have led us to think of nerves,and animal fpirits, or effluvia, becaufe the organs of fmell, do not refemble the fenfation of fmelling, nor does this fenfation refemble the objects from which the fmell, that is, the fenfation arifes, page 29.

The Dr. takes great pains to fhew,at p. 28, &c. that although men are poffeffed of the power, or faculty of fmelling ; yet that neither the organ of fmell, nor the medium (by which *it*, that is, the odour fmelled, is conveyed to that organ) nor any motions we can conceive in the *pituitary* membrane, or the *olfactory* nerves, or in the animal fpirits, do in the leaft *refemble* the *fenfation* of fmelling. How fubftances or motions can refemble fenfations, I muft own, I am not able to comprehend : as little can I comprehend the reafons for, or the benefits of, thefe obfervations which the Dr. thinks neceffary to premife, before he requefts his reader to attend to what the mind is *confcious* of, when we fmell a rofe or a lilly— But what if this confcioufnefs fhould prove a fallacy, for,to ufe the Dr. words, p. 12, who is voucher for confcioufnefs, and who can prove that his confcioufnefs does not deceive him? the Dr. goes on " fince our language affords no particular name for *that* perception in the mind, which arifes from the fmell of a *rofe* or a *lilly* (that is, fince we have not *particular* names for each *particular* fmell, but include agreeable fmells under the general name of *odours*, and difagreeable fmells, under the general name of *ftinks*) we call it a fmell or an odour—to be fure we do, for we cannot call it by a name which it has not got—well, and what then? why then the perfon who perceives this fmell cannot perceive any *fimilitude*, or *agreement*, between the fmell and the rofe, or indeed between this fmell, and any other object whatever. And what are we to conclude from this ?—Why " that the man cannot determine from the nature of the *thing* (of the fmell I fuppofe) whether *it* (the fmell namely) is caufed by body, or fpirit—by fomething near, or fomething at a diftance. It has no fimilitude to any thing elfe fo as to admit of a comparifon, and therefore he can conclude nothing from it, unlefs perhaps that there muft be fome unknown caufe of it. Figure, colour, extenfion, or any other quality of bodies cannot be afcribed to it." To be fure they cannot. Nor can thefe qualities be afcribed to found, to the fenfation of tafte, or to that of the touch, if we in both cafes regard the *fenfation only*, or in the Dr's. words, p. 28, " if we carefully exclude from thefe names every thing but the *fenfation itfelf*, nor can the perfon who perceives the fmell give it a *place*, the Doctor fays, p. 29, any more than he can give a *place* to melancholy and joy. Now what are we to underftand by giving a place to a fmell? Does the Doctor mean by this ftrange expreffion that fmells are incapable of, or inconfiftent with locality ? no general ideas are capable of locality ; but particular ideas are, and always muft be accompanied with the idea of locality. The tuberofe, which the Doctor fmelled, p. 30, was in a *certain* room, and the perfume it gave was in *that* room. But the Doctor confounds the power of perceiving odours or stinks, with the odours and stinks themselves. The *power* of *perception*, whatever be the thing perceived, is, and can only be in the mind that perceives it ; or according to the Doctor's expreffion p. 29, fenfation can only be in the *fentient thing:* but a power of exciting fuch fenfation, may be in things which are not fentient. And did not certain powers, regularly and generally accompany certain objects, the whole benefit of experience, by which alone men are fitted to live in this world would be utterly deftroyed. And what do we learn from thefe abftract obfervations as the Doctor calls them ? p. 30. "Why that fmelling (that is the power of fmelling) is a fimple original affection, or feeling of the mind, altogether inexplicable, and unaccountable, p. 31." And may not the fame thing be faid of all thofe perceptions, which are introduced into the mind, through the fenfes, and perhaps of all other perceptions? but furely all thefe philofophical obfervations were not wanted to prove what common fenfe difcerns at firft fight, viz. that we are utterly ignorant of the manner in which external objects act upon the fenfes, as well as the manner in which the information received through the fenfes is conveyed to the mind. And what is the upfhot of all the Doctor's laborious argumentation? why that we cannot afcertain by *reafoning*, that knowledge which is *wholly* founded in *experience*. But fo it is, becaufe theDoctor's countryman, Mr. Hume has written a great deal of what is either utterly confufed, or utterly unintelligible upon thefe fubjects, the Doctor kindly endeavours to father all this nonfenfe upon Mr. Locke : with what juftice all who are capable of underftanding Mr. Locke muft be able to fee. But however much the Doctor may reprobate his country-man, he writes with as little meaning and as much obfcurity himfelf.

If the Doctor seems little acquainted with the nature and the operations of our mental faculties, he seems equally ignorant of the nature and of the operation of our corporeal senses; and so he says when I smell a rose, I am necessarily determined to *believe* (I certainly know he should have said) that the sensation exists: that is, when the Doctor smells a rose he is necessarily determined to believe that he smells it.— Very wonderful this discovery! It is, the Doctor says, common to all sensations that they cannot exist without being perceived: that is, that they cannot be perceived, without being perceived; and, if they are perceived, what then? Why then they are perceived: for a sensation can only be in the sentient *thing*. Another discovery equally wonderful. And he tells us, Chap. ii. sect. 3. that a sensation, a *smell* for instance, may be presented to the mind three different ways.

I. It may be smelled.

II. It may be remembered.

III. It may be imagined, or thought of.

Now what are we to understand by a sensation being *presented?* But this is by no means the only place in which the Doctor's nonsense lurks securely under the covert of an indistinct expression, whenever his readers have not sagacity enough to discover the game, nor dexterity enough to beat the bush sufficiently to force it out of its hiding place. Had the Doctor been provided with understanding to perceive the truth, or honesty to avow it, he would not have used that ambiguous word presented, but have clearly and fairly said, a sensation may be *excited* (for though objects may be presented to the mind, it can scarcely, with propriety, be said that sensation can) three ways: but then his favourite common fenfe would have told him, that *no* recollection of a *paft* fenfation will excite that fenfation *afrefh*, nor any imagination of it, or any thought about it bring back a *paft*, and caufe it to become a *prefent* feeling; for if it could, the effects of the external objects upon the fenfes, might be rendered perpetual; pain and pleafure would become capable of endlefs repetition by an *act* of the *will*, and one fmelling-bottle might ferve a nation : nor would it be true, as is always obferved, that the memory of paft fufferings is attended with pleafure, according to that of the Poet;

———— Dulce eft meminiffe laborum.

It is difficult, fays Dr. Reid, p. 26, to unravel the operations of the human underftanding, and to reduce *them* to their *firft* principles. Now what are we to underftand by the *firft* principles of the *operations* of the human underftanding? We cannot expect, the Doctor fays, to fucceed in the attempt (to unravel the operations of the human underftanding) but by beginning with the fimpleft, and proceeding to the more complex. Now what do thefe words, the fimpleft, and more complex refer to? not furely to principles, for who ever heard of *complex principles?* Or do thefe words refer to the operations of the human underftanding? for fo the Doctor fhould have worded it, if he had meant to be confiftent with what he had juft before written : but he had a different end in view, viz. that of introducing *unperceived* what he calls his principles of common fenfe, and fo he artfully fubftitutes the human *faculties* in the place of the human *underftanding*; well knowing that the word faculties is applicable to the *corporeal*, as well as to the *mental powers*, but that the operations of the human under-

ftanding relate to the powers of the *mind* ONLY; and
fo, having cunningly made this dextrous fhift, he goes
on with the moft affured confidence to inform his
reader, that in an Analyfis of the human *faculties* the
five fenfes may for *this reafon* (for what reafon?) *claim*
to be *firft* confidered; but had he honeftly put, what his
own affertions required, that in an Analyfis of the
human underftanding, the five fenfes claim to be firft
confidered, who but muft have feen that the *operations*
of the human mind, that is, of the intellectual faculties, are as different in their *nature*, as they are in their
purpofes, from *thofe* of the five fenfes? The external
fenfes are merely avenues, by which one fpecies of perceptions, viz. thofe which take their rife from objects
without the mind, are admitted into it.

The precedence in *this* confideration is to be given,
the Doctor tells us, not to the *nobleft*, or moft ufeful,
but to the *fimpleft* fenfe, which the Doctor deems to
be the fenfe of fmelling. But why fmelling is more
fimple than hearing, or tafting, we are not told; yet
the effects of thefe fenfes comprehend only one *fpecies*
of perceptions, viz, odours, or founds, or taftes.

Thofe who think it worth their while to examine
Dr. Reid's book, will find that it abounds with the
like precifion of ideas, and reafoning of a *fimilar* fort.
Perhaps much of this confufion would have been prevented, and much ufelefs argumentation faved, had
the Doctor not been fo fearful of defining; for whatever incredible paradoxes he might fuppofe to have
rifen from this practice, none furely can be more incredible than the imagination that the more ignorant
we are of the meaning of the words we ufe, the better
we fhould underftand them. Without any apprehen-
fions of thofe dreadful confequences at which the
Doctor is fo terribly alarmed, I fhall venture to afcer-

tain the precife fignification of fome words which muft neceffarily be ufed upon this fubject.

1. By memory then I mean that faculty of the mind, by which we are enabled to recall our *knowledge* of paft perceptions, whether attained by confcioufnefs, or fenfation : the exertion of this faculty, I call, re-collection.

2. By confcioufnefs I underftand that faculty of the mind by which we become acquainted with the opera-tions of our various intellectual powers, and the effects of thefe operations; alfo with the exertion of our af-fections and paffions, with our defires, and with thofe acts of the mind which we call intention, and defign, and with the acts of the will.

Thus we fee that memory relates chiefly to that knowledge which we *receive* from *external* objects; con-fcioufnefs to that knowledge which *arifes* from the action of our *own internal* powers. We cannot be con-fcious of the mental operations of *other* men, but we may remember their words or their actions, and may be confcious of this remembrance, as we are confcious of all other acts of our own minds. Memory can relate *only* to *paft* knowledge. Confcioufnefs may relate to the prefent as well as to the paft actions of our minds. We certainly remember what we have a *paft* confcioufnefs of, but the converfe is by no means true, that we are confcious of whatever we remember, yet this would have been the cafe had confcioufnefs and memory been, as Dr. Reid afferts, the *fame thing*.

3. By fenfation I mean that faculty of the mind, by which we became acquainted with the effects of exter-nal objects upon our corporeal fenfes.

4. By perception I underftand that *information* refpec-ting the *internal* acts of the mind, and the external ac-tions of objects upon the fenfes, which we receive by confcioufnefs or fenfation.—And

5. By ideas I understand the effects of thefe internal acts of our mind, and of external objects tranfmitted through our corporeal fenfes. So that ideas are not perceptions, but the confequences of them ; and with Dr. Reid's leave I muft beg to ufe this word, till I am furnifhed with a better reafon for laying it afide than any I can find in his book : for unlefs you admit this fpecies of intuitive knowledge, which we receive from the faculty of confcioufnefs, however inexplicable the nature of it may be (though perhaps not more fo than many other of our mental or corporeal faculties,) you deprive men of the character, both of *rational* and *moral* beings; fince this confcioufnefs of the internal acts of our intellectual powers, and of our moral difpofitions, is the great characteriftic diftinction, between mankind and the animal world.

It may be proper to obferve, that the word perception is fometimes ufed for *that* power of the mind by which it difcerns the various objects prefented to it, whether voluntarily or involuntarily. Sometimes for the *exertion* of this power, and fometimes for the *effect* produced by this exertion.

The information attained by the ufe of our perceptive power is either;

I. Acquired.—Or
II. Received.

When this information is derived from the *voluntary* exertion of our intellectual faculties, I fay that it is acquired. But when it is forced upon the mind by the involuntary emotions of the affections, and paffions, and defires ; or by the ufual and cuftomary action of external objects upon the fenfes, I fay it is received.

C

The information acquired by the voluntary exertion of our intellectual powers, is such as we owe to intuition, or demonstration. We cannot remember an intuitive truth, without being conscious of the intuition, whereby we know it to be such ; but we may remember that we have been *convinced* by a demonstration without being conscious of the various intuitive steps which led to that conviction. The last is the recollection of a past fact—the other is a present operation of the mind.

The following observations of Mr. Locke, B. I. Chap. ii. Sect. 7. are so strongly verified in the conduct of most serious persons (as they are now *technically* called) in these days, and the practice therein noticed so strongly encouraged by the religious teachers of *all* denominations, that I could not forbear quoting them. " With these persons, doubtful expressions, that have scarce any signification, go for *clear* reasons to those, who being *prepossessed*, take not the pains to examine even *what* they themselves say,"—For—" The great difference, Chap. iv. Sect. 22. that is to be found in the notions of mankind, is from the different use they put their faculties to ; whilst some (and those the most) taking things upon *trust*, misemploy their power of assent, by lazily enslaving their minds to the dictates, or dominion of others in doctrines which it is their duty carefully to examine, and not blindly, and implicitly to swallow." But though the *generality* can no more be expected to examine for themselves, than they can be expected to calculate an eclipse, yet the teachers of religion, those especially who have had an university education, may surely be expected to be well aware of the heinous crime of misleading others, through their own prejudices, or their own ignorance. Of the students from academies I say nothing, for such institutions *generally* profess to teach a great deal too much to afford a reasonable expectation, that persons educated in them, can possibly understand *any one* subject *accurately*.

Obſervation i. upon Book II. Chap. i. Sect. 10.

Our being ſenſible of *it* (i. e. of the exiſtence of ſome certain thing,) is not neceſſary to any thing (not neceſſary to the exiſtence of ſuch thing) but to the exiſtence of our thoughts; i. e. our being ſenſible of our thoughts, is neceſſary to *their* exiſtence—neceſſary to conſtitute them ſuch.

Obſervation ii. upon Book II. Chap. ii. Sect. 1.

It ſeems an inaccurate way of ſpeaking, to ſay that *ideas* are united in the ſame ſubject. Ideas (in the primary ſignification of the word) are merely ſenſations excited in the mind by the operation of external objects upon the corporeal ſenſes, and therefore, ſtrictly ſpeaking, can only be united in (i. e. combined by) the mind. The ſame object may indeed poſſeſs powers of ſuggeſting various ideas. See Obſervation iv. B. II. Chap. xxviii. xxix. xxx. xxxi. See alſo Chap. xxxii. Sect. 14, 16. & Book IV. Chap. iv. Sect. 4.

Obſervation iii. upon B. II. Chap. iv. Sect. 5.

Extenſion of *body*, ſays Mr. L. *is* the coheſion, or continuity of ſolid, ſeparable, moveable parts. The extenſion of body may be *owing* to the coheſion, and continuity of ſolid parts. But are not theſe ſolid parts extended ? and what is their extenſion owing to ? to the coheſion, and continuity of further ſolid parts ? and are we to ſay with the poet,

> So naturaliſts obſerve, a flea
> Hath ſmaller fleas that on him prey;
> And theſe have ſmaller fleaſt o bite'em,
> And ſo proceed ad infinitum.

But whatever extenfion of body may be owing to, it cannot be neceffary that the folid parts fhould be feparable, and moveable.

Mr. L. calls the extenfion of *fpace*, the continuity of *unfolid*, (furely not fluid) infeparable, immoveable parts. What are unfolid, infeparable, immoveable parts? Space is a general, or an abftract idea, and therefore *nothing*. Extenfion of fpace is a *negative* idea, it denotes the *abfence* of body, or matter. See Obfervation x.

Obfervation iv. upon B. II. Chap. viii.

Whenever objects, *however modified*, have a power of exciting the *fame* ideas, Mr. L. attributes this power to what he calls their *primary qualities*, and he afferts, Sect. 15, that the *ideas* of thefe primary qualities are *refemblances* ; that is, images of fuch primary qualities; for that *their* patterns (the patterns, namely, of thefe primary qualities) do really exift in the bodies themfelves. But when objects have the power of exciting *ideas*, which ideas have *no* fuch refemblance, or image, he attributes *this* power to what he calls their *fecondary qualities*.

Mr. L. feems to have been led into this notion of primary, and fecondary qualities, by not attending to the *difference* between ideas, and images. Images can only be received by the *fight*, they neither are, nor can be conveyed to the mind by any other fenfe, by the touch fuppofe, fee B. II. Chap. ix. Sect. 8. Dr. Reid indeed fuppofes that blind perfons may become poffeffed of images, as well as thofe who have the ufe of fight, though nothing can be plainer, than that they can only be received into the mind by the eye. Becaufe blind perfons can acquire the *idea* of a line, (for who has an image of a mathematical line, i. e. a line which has *no* breadth) and can underftand the various relations which arife from the pofitions of lines, with regard to each

other, and can conceive the ideas of folids, generated
by the revolution of plane figures about fome *given
line*, appertaining to fuch figure; the Doctor, therefore,
imagines that they may be enabled to form images of
external objects, as well as perfons who have the ufe of
fight. He might with equal reafon have imagined,
that becaufe blind perfons can conceive the *mathematical* relations of the rays of light confidered as lines, and
the mathematical generation (if I may fo call it) of the
rain-bow, that therefore they can acquire the idea of
colours. Upon what fort of ground the Doctor builds
all this notion, may be feen by that imagination of the
blind man, who fancied that fcarlet refembled the found
of a trumpet. But the Doctor goes further, and endeavours to prove, by a regular demonftration, the truth
of his affertion. The blind man is to conceive lines
drawn from the center of a fphere, through all the various points of an object of *touch* placed within the
fphere, and near to its internal furface ; and then lines
are to be drawn from the center of the fphere, through
all the various *(delineatory)* points of this object of touch,
to the internal furface of the fphere, and the points
where thefe radii *terminate* are to be *joined* ; and as thefe
lines *fo* joined, will become *circles* of the *fphere* the Doctor fuppofes a complete projection of the object, i. e.
a *true* image of it will be formed upon the internal furface of the fphere ; but fince a blind perfon can conceive the circles of the fphere, and fince thefe delineatory lines, are all circles of the fphere, therefore it is
plain, the Doctor fays, that this blind perfon will alfo
conceive the vifible image of the object *fo* drawn upon
it.

The Doctor is not aware that light and fhade (of
which a blind man cannot poffibly have any conception)
i. e. light in the different degrees of it, form a principal
part of thofe images which arife from the fight ; and

that unlefs the *delineatory* lines are projected upon a
plane at right-angles to the *principal* vifual ray, the image
will vary, more or lefs, from the real appearance, as
may be fully feen by the length of the fhadows of objects, made upon the ground by the fetting fun ; for in
this cafe the folar rays refemble the vifual ray, and the
ground the plane of projection. But the Doctor's ideas
upon the fubject, are as muddy as they are upon other
fubjects, or he would have known that an image made
according to the rules of perfpective upon a curve furface, must prefent a diftorted picture to the eye, as the
common optical cylinders fufficiently fhew. The fubject is of little importance, but the Doctor has exhi-
bited an enormous parade of mathematics, only to op-
pofe what he took to be the opinion of Mr. Locke,
with how much judgment, and to how much purpofe,
the reader of it muft determine. But to return to our
more immediate fubject. Mr. L. was not aware that
as foon as you feparate the parts of the image, i. e. the
different ideas of which the image is made up, the co
lour, fhape, fize of a bird fuppofe, you utterly deftroy
the refemblance, that is, the image in the mind, fuggefted by the *particular* object, from which fuch image
was received : for images are the refemblances of *particular* objects. There is no fuch thing as making, or
conceiving an image, which fhall refemble *all* birds, of
every fize, fhape, and colour, any more than you can
form a refemblance of folidity, extenfion, mobility,
divifibility, &c. And you may juft as well fay, that
the colour, fhape, fize, &c. exift in the object when
you do not fee them, as that the folidity, extenfion, &c.
exift in the object, when you do not perceive them.
To affirm this, is only to fay, that *fuch* objects have the
power of exciting fuch ideas, whenever thefe objects
occur to the fenfes ; and all objects have, and muft
have, this power of exciting ideas, or they would not be
objects at all.

The *idea* of folidity, extenfion, &c. taken without reference to body, or matter *actually* exifting, is nothing but an idea, and is no more in the body from whence it is received, than the idea of pain, or ficknefs, (fee Sect. 18.) is in the manna. To afk, as Dr. Reid does, " whether thefe perceptions are any *thing*, is to afk whether they are not *fomething elfe*, and *not* perceptions ? To afk whether they are *real*, is to afk whether in the *fame* circumftances, they occur to *all* mankind? To fuppofe it neceffary, as the Doctor does, that there fhould be a *fimilitude*, between every perception, and the circumftance from which fuch perception arifes, is to make a fuppofition, for which there is no general foundation : and in every cafe, but that of perceptions received by the fight, i. e. of images, the fuppofition is manifeftly impoffible. Matter has a power of exciting the ideas of folidity, and extenfion, and manna has a power of exciting the ideas of ficknefs, and pain. The former of thefe ideas can be admitted into the mind by the *touch* of the *hands*, the latter only by the *touch* of the *ftomach* ; but ideas are ftill ideas, by whatever way they are admitted, and *as* ideas, they are only *in* the *mind*, they neither are nor can be in the objects which excite them." (B. II. Chap. xxiii. Sect. 10.) The ideas themfelves, and the power of exciting thefe ideas, are very different matters. It feems indeed juft as poffible to explain the mode by which fenfation is produced in us, or the way by which external objects excite ideas in our minds, as it is to explain the nature of fleep, or of dreaming, the operation of recollection, or the beginning of motion in the body, in confequence of the action of the will.

Obfervation v. upon Book II. Chap. viii. Sect. 9.

What Mr. L. calls *qualities* in objects, is only the

exiſtence of powers in theſe objects to excite certain ideas, B. II. Chap. xxiii. Sect. 10, in our minds. But what are thoſe qualities which are ſo inſeparable from the body in which they exiſt, as not to admit of any *poſſible* change? The power of exciting certain ideas we ſay, is in the object,—but there are powers in other objects, which can totally deſtroy theſe *original* powers, and introduce new ones in their ſtead. Thus the action of fire, or of aqua regia, can give to gold a power of exciting another idea which it did not poſſeſs in its original form, viz. the idea of fluidity; and it takes away the power it before had of exciting the idea of ſolidity. So the action of the ſun takes from bees-wax, the power it had of exciting the idea of yellowneſs, and gives it a power it had not before, of exciting the idea of whiteneſs, and ſo on. We know of no matter whatever which is not liable to ſuch changes. Divide a piece of wood, Mr. Locke would ſay, yet ſtill each part has ſolidity, and extenſion; ſolidity, and extenſion are *therefore primary qualities*.—Put it into the fire, ſay I, and then what becomes of *theſe* primary qualities? will it ſtill retain them? Yet this is his grand criterion of ſuch qualities. Mr. L. is not aware, that when he talks of qualities that are utterly *inſeparable* from the body, in *what eſtate ſoever* it be, ſuch qualities, as in *all* the *alterations* and *changes* it ſuffers, and under *all* the *force* that can be uſed upon it, it conſtantly keeps; and when he inſtances in what he would *call* the *qualities* of extenſion, and ſolidity, and figure, &c. he is only reciting the *general* ideas which enter into his abſtract idea of matter, or ſubſtance, and which of courſe will always be found with the reſpective *particular* ideas, from which ſuch *general* ideas are taken, but never can be found without them; in the like way Mr. Dugald Stewart tells us, page 3, of his Philoſophy of the Human Mind, 8vo. 1802, " that the ideas annexed to the words matter, and

mind, (as he fays is well obferved by Dr. Reid, in his
Effays on the active powers of Man, p. 8 & 9,) are
merely *relative*." (I am not fure that I underftand what
he means by this word,) " if I am afked," he goes on,
" what I mean by *matter*, I can only explain myfelf by
faying it is *that* which is extended, figured, coloured,
moveable, hard or foft, rough or fmooth, hot or cold—
that is, I can *define* it no other way, than by enumerating its *fenfible qualities*. It is not *matter* or *body*, which
I perceive by my *fenfes*. To be fure not. Matter or
body is a general idea, the mere creature of the mind,
and created merely for the conveniency of *verbal* communication. When Mr. Stewart looks at his poultry—
it is not *bird* which he perceives by his fenfes, but cocks,
hens, chickens, ducks, geefe, and turkeys : ideas taken
from actual exiftence, can only be excited by particular
objects, but when we want to difcourfe about a great
number of particular objects, which fuggeft fome ideas
that are the *fame*, and alfo fome ideas that are *different*,
a *general* term comprehending them *all*, but *exactly*
agreeing to *no* one in particular, muft fave the trouble
of *refering* to each particular idea. Juft fo the chymifts
obferve, that phlogifton is never to be met with *pure*,—
and how fhould it ? for it is the *general* idea of *inflam-
mability :* but this idea cannot be an object of Senfe—
like all other general ideas, it is collected from obferving many different kinds of fubftances which *will* burn,
as well as many, which will *not* ; and it is this difference,
which gives rife to the general term in this cafe, as it
does in all others, for if *all* fubftances would burn, we
fhould have no occafion for *this* term; there would have
been no opportunity to diftinguifh between fuch matters as would burn, and fuch as would not. General
ideas are *fimple* ideas, they cannot be defined, we can
only refer to the manner in which they are *acquired*, in

order to communicate our knowledge of them to other perfons, they neither are, nor can be objects of fenfe. Objects of fenfe muft be *particular* from the very nature of them.

Obfervation vi. upon Book II. Chap. ix. Sect. 3.

Whatever impreffions are made on the *outward* parts (fenfes) if they are not taken notice of *within*, fays Mr. Locke, there is no perception; which is only faying, if there is no perception—there is no perception. Mr. Locke meant to have faid, that a certain degree of *attention* was neceffary, to render the action of external objects perceptible; and by attention, I mean the application of our various powers to their *appropriate* objects. But fuch is the nature of the human frame, that we cannot attend *equally* to two, or more objects at the *fame* time. All perfons can hear articulate founds, which are *familiar* to them, and which they *expect*, with much greater facility, than thofe to which they are intire ftrangers.

Obfervation vii. upon B. II. Chap. xii. Sect. 4.

" I call fuch ideas," fays Mr. Locke, "complex ideas, which however compounded contain not in them the fuppofition of *fubfifting* by themfelves,—but are confidered as dependencies on, or affections of fubftances." Now what are we to underftand by ideas *fubfifting* by themfelves? and what by their being *dependencies* on, or *affections* of fubftances? All ideas, except thofe formed by the mind within itfelf, are fuggefted, or excited, by *external* objects. Are we then to confider general, or abftract ideas as *fubfifting* by themfelves? and *images* of external objects, or ideas fuggefted by, or arifing from, animate, or inanimate matter, as *dependencies* on, or af-

fections of fubftances ? Mr. Locke confiders the ideas fignified by the words, triangle, gratitude, murder, &c. as dependencies on, or affections of fubftances. But thefe ideas are all general, or abftract ideas. They are the creation of the mind, and if they can be faid to depend upon *any* thing, it muft be upon the will of him who forms them, and who chufes *what* ideas he will combine together, and exprefs, by thefe *names*. The idea of a triangle does not imply that fuch triangle is ifofceles, or equilateral ; fcalene, or right angled ; acute, or obtufe angled ; though Mr. Locke calls this idea, B. III. Chap. iii. Sect. 9, a *thing*. The *image* indeed of a triangle does determine the *kind*, but then images are *particular* ideas, that is, they are the image of fome *particular* thing, B. IV. Chap. vii. Sect. 9.

Obfervation viii. upon Book II. Chap. xii. Sect. 6.

" The ideas of fubftances," fays Mr. Locke, " are fuch combinations of fimple ideas as are taken to *reprefent* particular things, that is, particular fubftances." The ideas of fubftances are *collections* of all thofe various fimple ideas, which fuch fubftances have a power of exciting : but what fort of a reprefentation is the reprefentation of folidity, mobility, divifibility, &c. ? But fays Mr. Locke, " along with thefe combinations of fimple ideas, the *fuppofed*, or *confufed* idea of fubftance, *fuch as it is*, is always the firft, or chief."—Here again, fubftance is a *general*, or *abftract* idea, and like all other general or abftract ideas, is no more confufed, than any other general, or abftract idea, of folidity, or mobility fuppofe. General or abftract ideas do not admit of *any image* in the mind, however they are made, and you have juft as clear an idea of fubftance as you have of animal, or creature, or human nature, &c.

Obſervation ix. upon B. II. Chap. xii. Sect. 13.

" The parts of *pure* ſpace," ſays Mr. Locke, " are *inſeparable*, *one* from the *other*; and again, Sect. 14, the parts of *pure* ſpace are immoveable."—The *parts* of an *abſtract* idea! He muſt be cunning who can *divide* an abſtract idea, or who can conceive the *motion* of it.

Ideas are the *materials* of all our knowledge. They are either,

I. Suggeſted to the mind by the various external objects, with which we are every where ſurrounded.—Or
II. They are formed by the mind within itſelf.

The *firſt* ſort of ideas are conveyed to the mind through the ſenſes, by the action of theſe various powers of the human body. The *ſecond* are formed by the mind itſelf, in conſequence of the action of the various powers of the human underſtanding; by which we are enabled at *will* to *compare*, *combine*, *ſeparate*, and *recall* our ideas; and in conſequence to *form* abſtract, or general ideas in the mind, for the convenience of language; images in the imagination for pleaſure; and alſo to combine a variety of *images*, and *ideas* by the faculty of invention, for the various purpoſes of life. Hence alſo we further obtain occaſion for exerciſing thoſe other operations of the mind, *attention*, *conſideration*, and *judgment*.

The ideas conveyed to the mind *through* the *ſenſes* are always of a *definite* kind, they are the ideas of *particular* objects, for they are excited by particular objects. Whenever ideas are excited by *ſuch* objects, as are not wholly within the reach of our ſenſes, whether from the magnitude of the object, the imperfection of our ſenſes, or from any other cauſe, theſe objects can be only *imperfectly* comprehended: the parts out of the reach of our

senses are just the same, with respect to us, as *no*
parts : in such circumstances, we have, and can only
have, a *partial*, that is, an *imperfect* idea ; and when the
parts out of the reach of our senses, are utterly *undisco-*
verable, as in the case of infinity, to whatever this term
is applied, the idea we have cannot be particular, i. e.
defined—it must be general. But it is impossible that
objects should excite *general* ideas. These *general* ideas
are, and can only be creatures of the mind, and therefore cannot be *marks*, like *particular* ideas of real ex-
istence.

The external objects, suggesting ideas to our minds,
differ greatly from each other ; and ideas suggested by
them, are admitted into the mind, by senses no less
different, according to the nature of the respective objects suggesting, and the nature of the ideas suggested
by them. These ideas sometimes arise from a *single*
perception, as is the case of smells, sounds, colours, &c.
sometimes they arise from a *number* of different perceptions, as in the case of many images, presented through
the eye, and of various substances, and kinds of matter from which we receive ideas by the touch. Some
ideas do *not* suggest the notion of parts, as colours,
sounds, smells, and tastes : some suggest the *notion* of
dissimilar parts, as those of substances, whether animate,
or inanimate ; and some suggest the notion of *similar*
parts, as the ideas of number, extension, and perhaps
that of duration. When complex ideas are made up
by the repeated addition of the *same simple idea*, as all
ideas of number, are made up of units, those of linear
extension of *particular* lines, &c. these simple ideas become *measures* of the collective ideas, and by means of
such measures, the various quantities of number, and
extension can be compared with each other respectively ;
and thus the relative proportion of each can be ascertained : for by comparing *magnitudes* with each other,

by means of some common measure, we acquire the idea of that *relation* which we call proportion : and as there neither *is*, nor can be any limits to *ideal* addition, or division, this ideal addition, or division, is said to be *infinite*. A word which does not imply any *positive* idea, B. II. Chap. xvii. Sect. 18, but only a *negation* of limits, to the perpetual repetition of *such* addition, or division. The same is true of the immensity of space, the infinity of number, the eternity of duration—they are mere negative ideas : but when space, number, or duration by being *defined* in *quantity*, become *particular*, and *therefore positive* ideas, they acquire the names of time, place and quantity. Yet Mr. Locke applies the *negative*, and *therefore* unattainable idea of infinity, B. II. Chap. xxiii. Sect. 34, & 35, to attain a precise, i. e. a positive idea of God. When we say that the power, wisdom, goodness, and knowledge, &c. of God are infinite, we mean to say, that we know *not how far they* extend. When immensity, eternity, spirituality, &c. are applied to God, these words are not intended to convey any positive idea *what* God *is*, but what he is *not*. The ideas of the immensity of space, the infinity of number, the eternity of duration, are not suggested to our minds by *any* objects *actually* existing, B. II. Chap. xvii. Sect. 4, & 5 ; they are *formed* by the mind : but the mind cannot *form*, it can only *receive* the ideas of the objects which *actually exist*, B. II. Chap. ii. Sect. 2. The ideas which the mind *forms*, neither are, nor can be ideas of things which actually exist, they are, and only can be general, i. e. abstract ideas. To say, as is sometimes said, that God is extended through the *whole* of infinite space, when the idea of *whole* cannot possibly be applied to infinity : to talk of the whole, of what, from its very nature, neither has, nor can have a *whole*, is to talk unintelligibly, is to use words which have no meaning. When we speak of the omnipresence, or ubiquity of God, we mean only, that he knows perfectly the state of, and changes in his own works, however diftant from each other, at all times, that nothing is unknown to him.

Obfervation x. upon Book II. Chap. xiv. Sect. 2.

Mr. Locke fuppofes the idea of duration may be acquired by obferving the fucceffion of ideas in our own minds. Perhaps it might be acquired more readily, by obferving the motion of two bodies (of which the fwifteft precedes) paffing along the *fame* line, with unequal velocity. Our ideas of the parts of duration are always referred to thofe meafures which the mind arbitarily applies to it ; for it feems not to have any natural meafure like extenfion, and number. Its parts cannot be *compared* with each other, like thofe of linear extenfion, number, or fome forms of fpace, by juxta pofition.

Obfervation xi. upon Book II. Chap. 21.

Defire I apprehend is a *ftate* of mind confequent upon the perception of fome good, *without* any confideration whether fuch good is attainable, or not. This confideration may precede, or follow, but makes *no* part of *fuch* ftate. Intention I fuppofe is a determination of the mind, refpecting *future* action, as volition refpects *prefent* action. I call *will* the *power* of *choice*. *This* power as *exifting* in the mind, implies from the very nature of it, the moft perfect freedom from *all* reftraint. I fay as exifting in the mind : becaufe the effects, (not the *action*) of this power may be hindered by external caufes. The thief in jail may *choofe* to be at large, and no power on earth can hinder his *choice*, though it may prevent the *execution* of that choice. The man's will is no lefs free, although his body may be bound in chains, and his limbs in links of iron ; any more than he lofes the *power* of *fight*, though he choofes to fhut his eyes, or is confined in a dark cell, where he can fee nothing : the effect of that power is indeed hindered pro tempore, by thefe external reftraints. When God, by a voice from heaven, prevented Abraham from flaying his fon, the action was as effectually hindered, as if the patriarch had *chofen* to difobey the divine command, given to facrifice Ifaac, or God had ftruck him with a dead palfy when he ftretched forth *his hand to compleat* the facrifice. It would have been equally compleat, though not to human eyes, if by a band of robbers, Ifaac had been carried away during the journey, *to the place of facrifice.* And God, who feeth not as man feeth, might with equal truth have pronounced the obedience of Abraham perfect in the fame words, " for becaufe thou *haft done* this thing, and haft *not* withheld thy fon—thine only fon, &c." Nobody, however, calls *external* hindrances, *neceffity.* That reftraint alone is neceffity, which takes away the *power*, not that which only prevents the wifhed for effect of choice.

Obfervation xii. upon Book II. Chap. xxi. Sect. 13.

Agents that have *no* thought—*no* volition—*no* power of choice—are—*no agents.* Such beings are *paffive*, not active beings. Thofe motions of the parts of the body, which the will can neither excite, nor prevent, are, fo long as this inability continues, neceffary motions ; *i. e.* they are fuch for which the perfon is not refponfible. It is the power of choice which makes agents refponfible for their actions.

Obfervation xiii. upon B. II. Chap. xxi. Sect. 15, & 16.

Mr. Locke confounds the *freedom* of choice, with

the *power* of *acting* in confequence of that choice. If you define *will* to be the power of choice, and *liberty* the power of acting in confequence of that choice, you make two diftinct powers ; volition belongs to one, and ability of action to the other.

Obfervation xiv. upon Book II. Chap. xxi. Sect. 17.

It is furely a ftrange thing to call the acts of choofing and perceiving, *modes* of *thinking*. Choice may depend upon *thought*; i. e. upon reflecting and confidering : and fight may depend upon choice. But feeing is no more choofing, than thinking is choofing, and choice is no more thinking than it is feeing, or recollecting. Thinking, and choice are two different operations of the mind, and as diftinct from each other, as invention and memory. The *will* certainly directs the operations of the underftanding, juft as much as it does the actions of the body ; were it not fo, a man might employ his judgment, when he fhould employ his imagination, and his legs, when he fhould ufe his hands.

Obfervation xv. upon B. II. Chap. xxi. Sect. 20, 21, 22, 23, 24.

The human mind is poffeffed, or confifts of a great variety of *powers*, no lefs *different* in their nature, than *diftinct* in the mode of their operations ; and by confidering the nature, and operations of each, we attain exact notions of the different forts of knowledge, which the mind is capable of acquiring ; and alfo of the manner, by which *each* fort is acquired : and there is no more impropriety in affirming, that the powers of perception, attention, confideration, judgment, imagination, invention, memory, &c. are feparate, and diftinct

E

faculties, than that fight, hearing, fmelling, tafting, feeling, are feparate, and diftinct fenfes of the body. Nor is it more abfurd to fay, that difcernment depends upon the power of perception, than that volition depends upon the power of choice. And to fay that the will is *not* free, becaufe a man muft receive, or reject what is thus propofed to his choice, is juft as wife as to fay, that a man is not free to fee *no* objects at all, when his eyes are open, nor free to fee any, when they are fhut.

Obfervation xvi. upon B. II. Chap. xxi. Sect. 28, & 29.

When Mr. Locke attempts to define volition, which, like moft acts of the mind, is a *fimple* idea (fee Sect. 30,) he is forced to define motion to be (if neceffity requires) *no* motion at all—i. e. freedom from motion, that is *reft*. He goes on to inquire, what determines the will? Had he attended, I do not fay to the *nature*, but to the *defign* of our various faculties, he would have feen that the inquiry was not lefs ufelefs, than abfurd. Indeed he feems to confound the power of choice, which God has given men (juft as he has given them the powers of perception, and fight, &c.) with the *particular* reafons for exercifing, i. e. for ufing thefe various powers. He alfo confounds the power of choice, which he calls preference, with the power of acting in confequence of this choice, as was before obferved. He confiders liberty, Sect. 8, & 24, or freedom, Sect. 27, not as the power of choice, but as the power of acting in confequence of this power of choice. But there is a manifeft difference. The power of choice, from the very *nature* of it, admits of *no* reftraint in *any cafe*. Men have no longer the power of choice, if this power *can* be *reftrained :* but the power of *acting*, may depend upon external circumftances in particular cafes. See Obfervation xi, & xiii.

Obſervation xvii. upon B. II. Chap. xxi. Sect. 30.

Mr. Locke cautions his readers not to confound deſire, and volition. They are as diſtinct, as deſire, and intention. Attentive perſons will ſee that deſire may reſpect *general* objects, choice (which is the action of the will) can only regard particulars.

Obſervation xviii. upon Book II. Chap. xxi. Sect. 31.

The *moſt* preſſing uneaſineſs, ſays Mr. Locke, determines the will ; i. e. he *calls that* uneaſineſs the *moſt* preſſing which *does* determine the will. All this is juſt like the final perſeverance of the ſaints.—All *who* perſevere are *ſaints*—And all *who* are *ſaints* perſevere—2d. edit.

Obſervation xix. upon B. II. Chap. xxiii. Sect. 15.

It is curious to ſee how a man of Mr. Locke's diſcernment, and warineſs, can put the change (to uſe a gallicism) upon himſelf. " Putting together, ſays he, the ideas of thinking, and willing, or the power of moving, or quieting motion, joined to ſubſtance, of which we have no diſtinct or poſitive idea"—i. e. no idea at all.—Now had this aſſertion been honeſtly worded, it would have run thus—putting together the ideas of thinking, and willing, or the idea to excite, or to quiet motion, to the idea of ſubſtance, of which we have *no idea at all*, we acquire, &c. A very curious mixture this of ideas, and no ideas !

Obſervation xx. upon Book II. Chap. xxiii. Sect. 18.

It is not true, that the ideas belonging to ſpirit, are *thinking*, and *will*; or a power of putting *body* (i. e. matter in general) into motion *by* thought. According to all our experience, spirit must be connected with body in a very peculiar manner, before it can produce motion *by* thought. Men can only move the parts of their *own* bodies *by* thought : to move *other* bodies, some what *more* than thought is necessary.

Observation xxi. upon B. II. Chap. xxiii. Sect. 30.

" The idea *we have* of spirit," says Mr. Locke—we have—we can have *no idea* of spirit—no *positive* idea. All we mean, all we *can* mean by this word, is only a negation of such sort of matter as we are acquainted with : and negative ideas cannot produce actual, i. e. *positive* knowledge. But, says Mr. Locke, " the substance of spirit is unknown to us—so is the substance of body equally unknown to us."—Very true to be sure. But matter suggests to us various ideas, through the senses, and it is by the senses *alone*, that we acquire the idea of real existence. A *power* of thinking, or acting is *no* object of our senses ; and though these powers are not found in any such sort of matter, as is the object of our senses, yet the *absence* of *these* powers from all *such* matter, as *we* are *acquainted* with, by no means shews the *nature* of *that* matter in which *these* powers are found. The word *immateriality* means only a negation of all such ideas, as are excited in our minds by substance. See B. IV. Chap. x. Sect. 13, 14, 15. & Chap. xi. Sect. 12.

Mr. Locke calls believing, doubting, intending, fearing, hoping, several *modes* of *thinking*. He might just as well have called expecting, admiring, loving, hating, modes of thinking.—It puts one in mind of the honest sea-lieutenant—" if any man contradicts me, I knock him down, that's *my way* of thinking."

Obſervation xxii. upon B. II. Chap. xxiv.

What Mr. Locke calls collective ideas, are only *ſuch* ideas to which number is applicable.

Obſervation xxiii. upon B. II. Chap. xxviii.

Mr. Locke writes a long, unintelligible chapter upon perſonal identity, to inquire in what identity conſiſts. It is unqueſtionably a perception of the mind, and you might juſt as well inquire, in *what* equality, or proportion, or the moral perception of right and wrong, conſiſts. Or, are you inclined to aſk, from *whence* this perception ariſes ? You may juſt as well aſk from *whence* all thoſe perceptions ariſe, which we call conſciouſneſs ? Indeed the whole moral government of God is, and muſt be founded in the identity of his intelligent creatures. To ſuppoſe a reſponſible being may *vary* from itſelf, is juſt as wiſe as to ſuppoſe that beings may contract guilt *before* they come into exiſtence ; or may commit crimes, *before* they are born. Yet however impoſſible, or abſurd theſe laſt notions may be, we know that many perſons, of the *reality* of whoſe piety no doubt can be entertained, have zealouſly maintained them. It is amongſt ſuch perſons, that we hear of ſinners by *nature*, and ſinners by *practice* ; a diſtinction not to be met with in ſcripture : and had theſe good perſons conſidered, what is, and only can be meant by the word *nature*, viz. that combination of powers, diſpoſitions, qualifications, and qualities which God has *allotted* to the various beings and matters which he has created, they would have ſeen the folly of this diſtinction. For, according to the information of that underſtanding which our Creator has given us, he can no more *make* or appoint men to be ſinners, independent of their own choice, than he can make the united ideas of two and three, to compose the idea of six; or than he can make a circle to have the properties of a triangle. According to all those ideas of justice which he has enabled us to collect, there cannot be *guilt* without *intention* and *design*, i. e. without the exercise of the *will* : where there is no guilt there can be no transgression, and consequently *no* punishment, in the *proper* sense of the word, for by punishment is meant evil inflicted, for evil done. All that this absurd distinction does, if we have any ideas to our words, is to make God the author of sin. But had men listened to that reason which God has given them, we should never have heard of such notions, or such inquiries.

It is curious to see what sort of reasoning, even able men are given to employ, when they must needs inquire into what cannot be understood. At Sect. 9, Mr. Locke defines person to mean a *thinking, intelligent* being, that has reason and reflection ; (are there then any thinking, intelligent beings, which have not reason and reflection ?) and can consider itself, as the *same* thinking *thing*, in different times and places. At Sect 11, he says, " thus we see the *substance* whereof personal-self, (i. e. person) consisted at one time, may be *varied* at another, *without* the change of personal identity ; there being no question about the same person," (i. e. the sameness of person) though the limbs, which but now were *part of it*, were cut off.—In these two passages, the word person is used for two *very different* ideas.

But this personal identity consists in a being, which is able to consider itself as the *same* thinking *thing*, in different times and places—that is—personal identity consists in being *able* to perceive it, or in other words, personal identity consists in—personal identity. Waving then all debate about the essence of personal identity, a doubt concerning which the ablest physicians have long held to be the *surest* mark of lunacy ; and of which es-

fence we fhall be hard fet to find a better criterion than
that of the Poet—

> If I be I, as I think I be,
> I have a Lifle dog that will know me:
> For if I be I, he will wag his tail,
> But if I b'ent I, he will bark and rail:

Obfervation xxiv. upon B. II. Chap.xxix . Sect. 4.

In enumerating the occafions of indiftinct ideas, Mr.
Locke omits one common caufe, viz. the attempting
to convey *fimple* ideas by *language*, whether it be by literal, or metaphorical defcription.

Obfervation xxv. upon B. II. Chap. xxix. Sect. 13.

Complex ideas, fays Mr. Locke, being made up of a
number, or collection of fimple ideas may be diftinct
in *one* part, and confufed in *another*. He inftances, in
the idea of a folid (and he might have inftanced, in
that of a plain figure) of a thoufand fides. The *idea*,
fays he, of the *number* is *diftinct*, that of the *figure* is confufed. He here confounds ideas and images. The
image of a figure of three or four fides, is as diftinct as
the ideas of the number three, or the number four: it
is the multitude of the fides that render the *idea* of the
image indiftinct. While numbers continue to be un-
applied to any particular fubjects, the ideas excited by
the *names* of fuch numbers, are only general ideas.
The words two—three—three dozen—three fcore—
three hundred, convey no ideas, till joined to fome fubject capable of number. They are indeed *precife* names,
and admit of *no* degrees, like many other fimple ideas;
and when applied can be *diftinctly* afcertained. The
mind can clearly conceive a fmall number of objects to
which number can be applied, but the diftinctnefs of

this idea is loft in a multitude; and, therefore, what Mr. Locke calls collective ideas, are a fort of general ideas —ideas, to be *precife*, muft be particular ideas.

Obfervation xxvi. upon B. II. Chap. xxx.

Our ideas are of two forts—They are either,

I. Such as are introduced into the mind through the fenfes, being the effects of powers implanted in the various works of God, and ordained by him to raife thefe fenfations in us—Or they are,

II. Modifications of thefe *original* ideas, and are the productions of our own minds, in confequence of the voluntary exercife of our various intellectual powers, and therefore may, perhaps, be more properly called *primary* and *fecondary*, or *native*, and *factitious* ideas, (primary, or native, as fuggefted, or excited, by the works of nature, i. e. of God : and fecondary, or factitious, as not being *originally received*, but being the voluntary productions of our minds,) rather than real and fantaftical : becaufe *all* our ideas are equally *real*, though not equally marks of real exiftence. And we conclude certain ideas to be *marks* of *real* exiftence, fince when men have the perfect ufe of thofe fenfes, through which *thefe* ideas are admitted into the mind, *they* appear to be *alike* in *all* mankind. And we reafonably conclude that the powers, by which objects excite *thefe* ideas, to be *permanent*, becaufe upon the *uniformity* and *regularity* of caufes, and effects, not only the comfortable fubfiftence, but the very exiftence of mankind does, in their prefent circumftances, and unavoidably muft, depend.

Obfervation xxvii. upon B. II. Chap. xxx. Sect. 2.

" Our fimple ideas," fays Mr. Locke, " are all *real*,

and *true*, becaufe they anfwer and agree to thofe powers of things which produce them." We *believe* thefe
ideas, as far as we can judge, are the *effects* of fuch
powers, and we *believe* the exiftence of fuch powers, becaufe *thefe* ideas are excited by *thefe* things, in the minds
of *all* mankind : and we conclude from the uniformity,
and regularity of *this* effect, that *the things* conftantly,
and univerfally exciting fuch ideas, are *real*, i. e. actually
exift.

Obfervation xxviii. upon B. II. Chap. xxx. Sect. 4.

Mixed modes and relations, fays Mr. Locke, have
no *other* reality, but what they have in the minds of
men, i. e. they are *mere* ideas. As *fimple* ideas are fuggefted to the mind by the works of God, fo the ideas,
called mixed modes, or relations, are fuggefted to the
mind by the *actions* of men, both through the fenfes,
and by reflection; juft as the knowledge of the exiftence
of God is fuggefted by his works through the fenfes, or
communicated by his word through the underftanding
to mankind.

Thefe ideas, (i. e. mixed modes) fays Mr. Locke, are
themfelves archetypes, and therefore cannot differ from
their archetypes, nor be chimerical, unlefs any one will
jumble together inconfiftent ideas (as Jofeph Milner,
and Bifhop Hoadley, have jumbled together the inconfiftent ideas of pardon and acquittal, fee Hoadley's
Terms of Acceptance, and the Differtation prefixed to
Four Effays, by T. Ludlam.) But Chap. xxxi. Sect. 3,
Mr. Locke fays, our complex ideas of modes, are voluntary collections of fimple ideas, which the mind puts
together, *without* any reference to *real* archetypes, or
ftanding patterns ; (a few lines lower he fays, mixed
modes, and relations *are* archetypes *without* patterns)

F

becaufe not being intended for copies of *things really* exifting, but for archetypes *made* by the mind. Is it proper to talk of archetypes *made* by the mind? If an archetype means any thing, it means a pattern, or fimilitude, to which recourfe may be had by *all* men; and can fuch recourfe be had to archetypes formed in, or by the mind, for the purpofe of comparing it with what is fuppofed to be fimilar? Complex ideas can only be communicated by definitions, i e. by enumerations of *all* the fimple ideas they contain, which are combined under one name, Book III. Chap. xii. Sect. 15, 16.

Obfervation xxix. upon Book II. Chap. xxx. Sect. 7.

If the effence of things is intelligible, it can only be known from an enumeration of that *whole* collection of powers to excite certain ideas, which are ufually found combined together in fuch things ; each of *thefe* powers are called *qualities*, or *properties*; but properties mean only a *partial* confideration of *fuch* things. *Nominal* effences are therefore nothing, B. III. Chap. iii. Sect. 15. Chap. iv. Sect. 3. Chap. viii. Sect. 1. Chap. ix. Sect. 17. Mr. Locke fays, B. III. Chap. v. Sect. 2, that abftract ideas are the *effences* of mixed modes. Abftract ideas are *nothing*, i. e. they have, they can have no connection with real exiftence, but are only general names. Mixed modes, fays Mr. Locke, are only made by the mind—they are made *arbitrarily*, i. e. without patterns. See Obfervation xxix. It is not true, as Mr. Locke fays, that mixed modes are made *without any* reference to *real* exiftence. They are made from obferving the actions of, and the relations interceding between men and each other, and between themfelves and their own actions.

Obſervation xxx. upon B. II. Chap. xxxi. Sect. 1.

When Mr. Locke ſays ſuch ideas are inadequate, which are partial, or imperfect *repreſentations* of the archetypes to which they are referred, he muſt be un-derſtood to ſpeak of *images*.

Obſervation i. upon Book III. Chap. vi. Sect. 28.

" It is neceſſary," ſays Mr. Locke, " to the making any nominal eſſence, i. e. any *ſpecific* idea, that the ideas, whereof it conſiſts, have *ſuch* an *union* as to make but *one* idea how compounded ſoever. *Such union* may, to be ſure, have *one name* ; but how it can become *one idea* I am not able to underſtand. Mr. Locke means, I ſup-poſe, that the ſpecific idea of ſubſtances, muſt be made up of *all* thoſe ideas which are ſuggeſted by ſuch ſub-ſtances reſpectively. The ſpecific ideas of mixed modes, ſo far as they are arbitrary, cannot be *falſe* ; but when we are to aſcertain the ideas annexed to words, which are uſed in *writers*, to *whom* we cannot have re-courſe for any deſired explanation, we can only collect theſe ideas from *their* uſe of words, conveying theſe ideas in different parts of their writings. The ſpecific ideas of ſubſtances are in *no* caſe arbitrary ; they muſt not contain any ideas which are not ſuggeſted by ſuch ſubſtances, he who ſhould put malleability into his idea of glaſs, or fixity in the fire, into his idea of ſteel, would give a *falſe* idea of theſe ſubſtances.

For an illuſtration of Book III. Chap. ix. Sect. 9. See the following

ESSAY UPON THE COMMUNICATION OF KNOWLEDGE.

The various faculties of the human frame plainly ſhew, that man was intended by his Creator to acquire

a variety of knowledge; and the organs of speech
vouchsafed unto him, as plainly shew, that it was also
intended, that he should communicate this knowledge
to his fellow-creatures. Because, to what purpose was he
thus qualified to make an endless *variety* of articulate,
i. e. distinct sounds, (a power *not* vouchsafed to any
other creature) and also to repeat with exactness these
specific sounds, as often as he chooses ; unless thes⸱
sounds were intended to be made signs of the ideas
which pass through his mind, and so to become means
of communicating to each other the knowledge possessed
by each individual.

But men are no less plainly intended for *social* life, and
the principal benefits of such a mode of living *can only*
arise from the *mutual* communication of knowledge :
but without a ready mode of such communication, the
benefits of society would be in a great measure lost, as
is plain from that very confined sort of it, which obtains
amongst the lower orders of living creatures. When
therefore such articulate sounds are *invariably* connected
with certain ideas, they become unequivocal *marks*, or
signs of these particular ideas ; and thus we are enabled
to make known to other men the ideas which exist in
our own minds. And when *visible* marks are used to
denote, either simple sounds, as in the letters of the
alphabet, or combinations of these sounds, as in the
Chinese characters ; each of which represents *not* an *idea*
(as is, I believe, often thought) but denotes combined
sounds, suggesting, like our words, a particular idea,
then we have every thing necessary for the construction
of language.

The sensations excited in the mind by external objects
are of two sorts,

I. Such as are excited by the objects themselves, and,
II. Such as are excited by *changes* in these objects—

and the various *modes* of these changes form an endless
variety of ideas, and occasion endless relations between
the words used to express the modes of these changes. *

* The application of *visible* words, or audible sounds to express
constantly some certain ideas must be *arbitrary:* because words or
sounds have in general no kind of connection with the ideas they are
usually chosen to express. But though *this* circumstance of language is plainly *arbitrary*, yet the *nature* of *it*, as far as regards the
relations of words to each other, must unquestionably arise from the
original relations of the ideas to be expressed.

Now the first application of *single* words, would naturally be to
express the *existence* of external objects, and accordingly the word
allotted for this purpose has usually been called the *nominative* case
of such word. The *involuntary* use of the corporeal senses would
suggest the existence of a great variety of objects, but the knowledge
of the relations of these objects to each other, that is, the different
powers possessed by them, of producing changes in each other, would
require greater attention to, and more extended acquaintance with
them. Men would distinguish between the objects which *produced*
these various changes, and those *in which* these changes *were* produced,
and this *difference* would suggest the notion of *active* and *passive* powers, as they are called : and the observation of instances in which the
exertion of power produced a change only in the object itself, and
not in any other, would give rise to the idea expressed by the *middle*
verb in the greek, (an idea between agent and patient, or rather made
up of both) the reciprocal verbs in modern languages ; and hence also
the idea of the *neuter*, in both ancient and modern, would naturally
arise.

The powers of producing changes, which were observed to be
constant and uniform, would naturally be supposed to reside in the
object, and belong to, or be possessed by it ; and hence the notion
of the *genitive* case in nouns. The change *produced* would be attributed to the operation of this power, which would be supposed to introduce, or effect such change, and *give*, as it were, this *new nature*
to the object changed, and hence would arise the idea of the *dative*
case. When the effect of the operation of these powers *was* to be
pointed out, or the agents exercising such powers were to be *denounced*, a case, (hence called the accusative case) is used : and when
these powers were observed to be taken from the objects in which
they were supposed usually to reside, and the instrument of this *de-
privation* was also observed ; words expressive of these circumstances, would of course constitute the *ablative* case ; and as instruments
of action must *accompany* the actor, the signification of *accompanying*

Now we can collect the nature of our ideas, and of the knowledge arifing from them, only by confidering

was alfo applied to *this* cafe. When particular men were wanted for particular purpofes, their attention would be excited by a *perfonal* addrefs, in what is hence called the *vocative* cafe.

To prevent an embarraffing multitude of words, wholly different from each other, the practice of prefixing fmall words, and transferring their fignification to the compound, or rather of combining the fignifications of *both*, took place; and the ideas annexed to each part of the compound, *flid* as it were into each other. A few inftances will explain my meaning. In the greek language, καλεω is to call, and αναχαλεω, to call *aloud* (to fpeak *up* as we fay) and as we call aloud to perfons at a diftance, when we wifh them to hear us, it fignifies to *recall:* and when things, which being worn, or broken, are by being repaired, *recalled* as much as poffible into their *former* ftate, this fame word fignifies to *mend*. Thus again φερω is to bring, καταφερω to bring *down*, and, as in ftriking the arm is brought down, it alfo fignifies to *ftrike*. And thefe *derivative* fignifications, are fometimes directly oppofite to the fenfe from which they take their rife. Thus ιςημι is to fet, or place, and ανιςημι to fet *up*, hence it fignifies to *build;* and as buildings are then moft compleatly deftroyed when their very foundations are raifed (razed) up, it alfo fignifies to pull down. Thus again the propofition Δια fignifies *through:* and as when things are pierced through, they are *completely* divided, when joined to the verb λαμβανω to take, it fignifies to fhare, i. e. to *divide* into fhares; and fo Plutarch tells us that at the funeral of Paulus Emilius, the ftrong young men, διαλαβοντις το λεχος, carried it to the grave, *dividing* fharing the load, equally, i. e. *completely* amongft them. So again defcribing the attack of Philopœmen upon Machanidas, each being on horfeback, he fays that Philopœmen (not λαβων but) διαλαβων τοιξυφον—taking his javelin or lance by the centre of gravity, dividing the weight equally in his hand, that is *poizing* his weapon. Here the fimple word λαβων would not have conveyed that *image*, or picture of the combat, which the writer fo graphically defcribes.

That a combination of two or more words into one was intended to change the fignification of the *fimple* word, none can doubt, for otherwife, why make this addition to it? When then we fee tranflators paying no regard to fuch addition, but preferving the fignification of the uncompounded word, we may have much reafon to fufpect that they do not give us the *true*, or the *full* fenfe of the paffage, and then we fhould always examine for ourfelves. Thus, when St. Paul fpeaking to the Elders of the Ephefian church, reprefents himfelf as not withholding any information from them, which could be

the ways by which we become poffeffed of them : and
we can collect the relations of words to each other, only

ufeful for their furtherance in the faith, in order to ftrengthen his
own vindication, he not only recounts his own *public* and *private*
diligence, but he adds διαμαρτυρόμενος, both to Jews and Greeks repen-
tance towards God, and faith towards our Lord Jefus Chrift. Beza
faw that fome addition was wanting to ftrengthen the fenfe of the
fimple verb μαρτύρομαι, and therefore tranflates it etiam atque etiam
teftificans. He was aware that the Apoftle meant an oppofition to ὐδὲν
ὑπεςειλάμην, τῶν συμφερὸν των; but he was not aware of the *peculiar force*
of the prepofition δια which is derived from the *compleatnefs* of that
divifion which is caufed by piercing any thing through and through,
as we commonly exprefs it. For this idea of *compleatnefs* which we
exprefs by the word *thoroughly*, attends this prepofition in inftances
where even the metaphorical fignification of it is quite inapplicable;
and fuch it is in the prefent cafe. Where it means not *fimply* teftify-
ing, but bringing fuch complezt, fuch *thorough* evidence of the truth
of what he taught as could not *poffibly*, that is, innocently be rejected.
And it may be obferved, that this fenfe clearly points out the force of
the apoftle's intended antithefis, between διαμαρτυρομαι & ὑποςελλομαι
for he might have teftified fome particulars *over* and *over again*, and
yet have not mentioned many of the τὰσυμφέροντα *to their conviction* ; nor have the different meanings of the prepofition δια, any the
leaft relation to the idea of repetition that I can difcover.

The following obfervations may further fhew the importance of
attending to the meaning of compound words. The doctrine of affurance as held by the Calvinifts, implying, as I collect from their
writings, not what the apoftle calls a lively hope, to which we are
led by the abundant evidence of the gofpel, but abfolute certainty
of our own falvation, and which is wholly founded upon their interpretation of the words πληροφορια and its derivatives. For all their
writers take what is delivered, without examination, from one
another, like the poet's hogs, " in huts of Weftphaly." According
to their expofition of πληροφορεω it means plenam fidem facio and
πληροφορεομαι plene perfuadeor—*certus* reddor: And the German
critic Stock, from whom this is taken, fays generatim notat *pleno
motu* in aliquid ferri—fpeciatim, proprie eft navium, quæ plenis velis
in portum feruntur—metaphorice eft animi qui pleno affenfu et
fiducia in aliquid fertur. The whole of this expofition is intirely
imaginary, and not at all grounded upon the real meaning of the
words. Πληροφορια, and πηροφορεω are compounded of the
words πληρης full, and φορεω to bear or carry, which is derived from
φορα a load, or burden, whatever is brought ; and πληροφορια means
a full load, fuch as was fuppofed to be the cargo of fhips, returning

by confidering the nature of the ideas they are intended
to exprefs. This knowledge of the relations of words to

to their own country, *deeply laden* with the produce of other nations ;
like bees to their hives, laden with wax and honey, the produce of
diftant flowers, as faft as they can : but the notion of fhips entering
their ports with *full* fail, is as far from real practice, as this critics
ideas are from thofe which are really annexed to this word ; for it is
always ufed in fcripture to exprefs, not the *ftrength* of the evidence,
but the *abundance* of it : becaufe it is of the *effence* of probable evidence to admit of augmentation, and hence we find the *degrees* of
faith continually noticed in the gofpel ; but certainty admits not of
degrees ; the information arifing from the *full* and *fair* evidence of
our fenfes, from intuition, and from demonftration, cannot be in-
creafed. *Twenty* different demonftrations of the fame propofition do
not make the truth of it a whit more certain than *one ;* but frefh
circumftances may increafe probable evidence, till the truth of it
becomes, not *certain* indeed, but utterly *indifputable* and *unqueftionable.* The gofpel might come with evidence, *wonderful* in its *nature,*
and *abundant* in *quantity,* as the Apoftle expreffes it, not in word only
but in (miraculous) power, and in the Holy Ghoft, and *therefore*
with much affurance ; but the affurance St. Paul fpeaks of here, is
what he elfewhere calls the full affurance of *hope :* he underftood too
well, though modern divines do not, the difference between the full
affurance of *hope,* and the full affurance of *certainty,* to confound thefe
utterly inconfiftent ftates of mind together, or to imagine them to be
the *fame ;* and fo he juftly obferves, that hope which is *feen,* i. e.
hope for the *reality* of whofe objects we have the *full* and *fair* evidence of *fenfe,* is not hope : becaufe whatever is the object of fenfe
is *certain,* but hope from the very nature of it implies *fome* uncertainty. With equal clearnefs and propriety he fpeaks of the *full* affurance of the underftanding ; that affurance, namely, which arifes
from underftanding the *nature,* and the *number* of the proofs of the
truths of the gofpel, which he fays came in full affurance, that is,
with unqueftionable evidence of its truth, though not with the conviction of demonftration. Thus the very argument ufed to prove
this *defirable* doctrine, *the certainty* of affurance, unanfwerably fhews
the thing to be impoffible : indeed the inconfiftency of thefe good
perfons is not a little remarkable, for while fome of them wifh to have
it thought that the proofs of the chriftian religion amount to abfolute
certainty, others of them are fearful that faith fhould be forced upon
them by mathematical demonftration. Knox's Chriftian Philofophy, page 42.

each other, conftitutes what we call grammar ; it has
its foundation in the conftitution of the human mind,
and in the conftruction of thofe organs which fit us for
intellectual communication, becaufe, in all languages,
modes of fpeaking are adopted, Euphoniæ gratia.

The human mind is enabled to receive immediate
knowledge refpecting the nature of and changes in the
material world—the actions of living creatures, and alfo
refpecting what paffes in the minds of *other* men, from
their information, communicated viva voce, or by
writing. Now the knowledge received through our
own *external* fenfes, when thefe fenfes are accurate,
muft be *true*, but the information received from *other*
men, *may* be falfe. Becaufe we can know exactly the
degree of accuracy of our *own* fenfes, and the degree of
care with which we have ufed them ; but we can neither
know the accuracy of the fenfes of other men, nor the
care with which they have ufed them, nor the ability,
integrity, or impartiality of the feveral perfons who may
have been employed in tranfmitting this knowledge :
upon all which circumftances, the truth of tranfmitted
information muft depend.

Befides the information received by *external perception*, (as that which we *receive* through our outward
fenfes, may not improperly be called) men are *confcious*
of the *exercife* and *application* of their own *internal* powers
(in confequence of the action of their own will :) this
latter kind of knowledge is wholly *perfonal*, it cannot be
acquired by any other man whatever ; it can *only* be *received* from the information of the individual who pof-
feffes it.

All thefe different forts of information excite in the
human mind various fenfations, and *thefe* fenfations I
call *ideas*; when thefe ideas are to be communicated to
other men, it can only be done by *words*, which are arbi-
G

trary marks of our internal fenfations, that is, figns of our various ideas, agreed upon by men for the purpofe of mutual intercourfe, and the mutual interchange of their refpective knowledge.

Now thefe *figns* of our ideas being wholly *arbitrary,* the accuracy of thefe figns muft intirely depend upon the care and exactnefs of him who ufes them. The uncertainty of language is often attributed to the imperfection of words, but it arifes much oftner from the imperfection, i. e. the negligence, inattention, or ignorance of him who ufes them; juft as the deceitfulnefs, and punifhment of fin, fo much infifted on by certain divines, means, in reality, the *difhonefty* and *punifhment* of *finners*. It is true that the mode of conftruction in *fome* languages is better adapted for precifion of expreffion, than it is in *others :* or what amounts to the fame thing, the relations of words to each other (upon the knowledge of which the exactnefs of language muft much depend) are capable of being afcertained, with *more* certainty in fome tongues than in others. This relation of words to each other conftitutes what is called the *idiom* of a language, and when writers in one language ufe the idiom of another, they render their own meaning utterly uncertain, unlefs they either give notice *when* they do fo, or invariably ufe a fixed mode of expreffing themfelves to convey the fame ideas; for then they form a language *peculiar* to themfelves. When then the connexion, between the *relative parts* of *fpeech*, is clearly and invariably pointed out, as it is in all languages in which the ufe of *genders* obtains, we cannot depart with fafety from the *ufual* fignification of the *general* idiom, to introduce and eftablifh a *particular* fenfe *inconfiftent* with it. For, if in any inftance you break through the *cuftomary* conftruction of language, without a better reafon than an imagination, that the interpretation you propofe conveys the weightieft and moſt natural ſenſe, by what *rule* ſhall any one know when we are to admit, and when to rejeᶜt the manifeſt intention of ſuch conſtruᶜtion ? Will not *every* man eſteem his *favourite* interpretation to be the *weightieſt*, and moſt *natural* ſenſe of the paſſage ? But without a better rule than the mere fancy of every man, will not the meaning of many paſſages of ſcripture become utterly uncertain.

Dr. Dodderidge, (in his note upon Eph. ii. 8. See his Family Expoſitor) in order to ſet aſide the authority of a very general, and very remarkable idiom, thinks it ſufficient to *aſſert*, that to underſtand the Apoſtle as affirming, that grace and the mode of that grace, is the gift of God, is to make the Apoſtle guilty of a flat tautology. Surely not more ſo, than when the ſame Apoſtle affirms, Tit. iii. 5. " that God ſaved us by his mercy, *not* by works of righteouſneſs which we have done." For if we are ſaved by the *divine mercy*, we cannot be ſaved by our *own* works, ſince mercy is compaſſion to the guilty, as pardon is deliverance from *juſt* puniſhment. Nor does this aſſertion involve tautology : for our ſalvation, i. e. deliverance from puniſhment, and admiſſion into heaven, might be received through the *favour*, the *grace* of *One*; and the intention of this benevolent deſign might originate in *Another*. And ſo we are told, that the ſalvation of ſinners was in conſequence of the eternal purpoſe of God the Father, which he purpoſed in *Himſelf*, and which he purpoſed to accompliſh in (i. e. by) Chriſt Jeſus. There is therefore *no* tautology in affirming that grace, and alſo the means of grace, *are* the gift of God.* The Doᶜtor goes on, " taking the

* It is a matter of the moſt awful, and painful concern to ſuch perſons as are truly deſirous to attain clear views (and who have been called in *ſcorn*, by the writers of the Chriſtian Obſerver, *Mathematical Divines)*—not of the divine reaſons for chuſing the *particular mode* of redemption *ſet forth* in the goſpel—nor of the *manner* in which

clause as we explain it, i. e. as afferting the *agency* of divine grace in the production of *faith, which* in his Comment he calls a *great* and *divine principle* in our *fouls,* the thought rifes, &c.—Now if inftead of this pious eulogy upon Faith, he had told us what he meant by *that* word, we fhould have been better able to judge of the truth of his affertions. For if by faith we are to underftand a firm belief, and well grounded perfuafion of the general truth of Chriftianity, founded upon that evidence which God has given for it ; how is receiving the truth, upon the evidence of faith, a more divine prin-

this mode has its *efficacy* (fee the groundlefs, and *therefore* foolifh explanations of thefe matters, in the writings of almoft all the ancient, and modern Calvinifts—becaufe of the *former* the Scriptures fay *nothing,* and only *fimply,* and *frequently affert* the latter) but of the *value* of this redemption, and of the obligations finners are under in the firft place to that *merciful* being; who, though he denounced death as the *certain* and *immediate* punifhment to the tranfgreffion of His command, Gen. ii. 17. was neverthelefs pleafed to fufpend the execution of his threatening (whether the wifdom of modern theologians can explain this feeming alteration of the divine counfels or not) and ftill continues to prefide over that gracious difpenfation, which originated *wholly,* and *only* in himfelf, Eph. i. 9. For without his *fpecial* agency, all that Chrift has done, or fuffered can profit men nothing. Since our Lord affures us, that *no* man can come unto him— can receive the benefit of his atonement and interceffion, except the *Father* draw him, John vi. 44. What fhall we fay then ? that we are under no obligation to the Redeemer ?—God forbid ! Great, and aftonifhing furely, was the generous benevolence of Jefus, who feconded the amazing love of the Father, and accomplifhed this great falvation at fuch an expence to Himfelf. For benevolence means only the defire of the happinefs of others, but generofity means promoting that happinefs at the expence of the promoter.

It is undoubtedly aftonifhing that any fhould neglect, or difregard the unfpeakable love and kindnefs of Jefus, but that any, who are fenfible of their obligations to him, fhould overlook, or difregard the no lefs unfpeakable love and kindnefs of the Father, from whom this gracious difpenfation took its rife, is ftill more aftonifhing. Becaufe it is only in confequence of the eternal purpofe of God, which he purpofed, *only,* and *folely* in Himfelf, that we have *acceptance* in the *beloved.*

ciple in the foul, than receiving it upon the evidence of demonftration, analogy, &c. ? You would not fay, that by knowledge is meant the effect of it. If you wifh to underftand by faith (what is indeed the *natural* confequence of it, i. e. *that* confequence which may *juftly* be expected from it) reliance, confidence, truft; you may juft as well underftand the words intuition, and demonftration to mean (what is indeed no lefs the natural confequence of them) certainty. (See an Effay upon the Nature of Faith, printed in the Orthodox Churchman's Magazine for November, 1802.) Indeed certain divines fpeak as if they thought, the *weaker* the evidence, the *more acceptable* to God the *act* of believing: they are very fearful, where no fear is, that faith fhould be *forced* upon them by *mathematical* demonftration, (Knox's Chriftian Philofophy, page 42, in the note, edit. 2.) Carry but this wife notion as far as it will go, and you will arrive at that celebrated maxim *Credo quia impoffibile.* We need not indeed wonder that little excellence fhould be attributed to the voluntary operations of our intellectual powers, fince even one of the warmeft, and moft amiable of the affections, and that temper of mind which is the natural confequence of it, and which is held not a little commendable amongft men, is very flightingly fpoken of, by much higher authority. If ye love thofe which love you, what thank have you? for finners alfo do the like.—The Doctor fays, as for the Apoftle's ufing τυτο in the *neuter* gender to fignify faith (πιϛις) the thing he had juft before mentioned, there are fo many *fimilar* inftances to be found in Scripture, that one would wonder how it were poffible for any judicious critics to have laid fo much ftrefs upon *this* as they do, in rejecting what *feems* beyond all comparifon, the *weightieft*, and moft *natural* interpretation. Now what are we to underftand by a *weighty* interpretation ? And do we not mean by a *natural* interpretation, such an interpretation as arifes from taking the words in their *common* and *ufual* acceptation, according to their grammatical conftruction? And might not one equally wonder how it were poffible for any judicious divines to have laid fo much ftrefs upon this *weightieft* and moft *natural* interpretation, without ever thinking of afcertaining the meaning of the words, or fhewing what they take to be the fenfe of them. To confirm the truth of *this* affertion the Doctor quotes Philip. i. 28. The words of the Apoftle are as follows: Καὶ μή πτυρόμενοι ἐν μηδενὶ ὑπὸ τῶν ἀντικειμένων· ἥτις αὐτοῖς μὲν ἐςὶν ἔνδειξις ἀπωλείας, ὑμῖν δὲ σωτηρίας, καὶ ΤΟΥΤΟ ἀπὸ Θεῦ. Alfo Eph. vi. 18. διὰ πάσης προσευχῆς καὶ δεήσεως προς εὐχομενοι ἐν παντὶ καιρῷ ἐν πνέυματι, καὶ εἰς ΑΥΤΟ ΤΟΥΤΟ ἀγρυπνᾶντες· And Galat. iii. 17. Τᾶτο δελέγω διαθηκην προκεκυρωμένην ἀπὸ τᾶ Θεᾶ εἰς Χριςὸν Ὁ μετὰ ἔτη, &c. Alfo iv. 19. τέκνια μᾶ ΟΥΣ. He might have added 2. Cor. ii. 6. and Apocal. ii. 15. He refers likewife to two celebrated fcripture critics, Elfner and Raphael, but he has not thought proper to adduce their obfervations in a matter, which might feem of fome importance, when he was endeavouring to eftablifh an interpretation, which, for aught appears, may be unintelligible, and not lefs oppofite to common fenfe, than to the rules of grammar. In fuch circum-ftances, one fhould have thought, a writer would avail himfelf of every thing he could : for not only the moft judicious critics, by whom he fets fo light, grammari-ans in general, are fo fenfible of the ufefulnefs of pre-ferving the uniformity and regularity of the eftablifhed conftruction of language, that they conftantly, and univerfally adhere to the cuftomary rules, as the only way of afcertaining, and rendering permanent the in-formation conveyed by, and received from it. Where-ever therefore thefe apparently anomalous conftructions are to be met with, they univerfally refer them to an elliptical expreffion, or a propofitional antecedent. For propofitions can be the predicate of other propofitions; and how numerous foever thefe irregular conftructions may be, you are not authorifed by their frequency to violate the general analogy of grammar, unlefs you can fhew that the referring thefe expreffions to an ellipfe, or a propofitional antecedent renders the fentence, in which they are found, unintelligible.

Had Doctor Dodderidge attended to the accuracy of St. Paul's language, rather than to his *own* fyftem of divinity, he would have feen that the Apoftle was fufficiently careful of precifion in his ftyle : for he might have noticed, in the very verfe quoted from Philipians, that in the fecond claufe St. Paul ufes ήτις (which faith) not ότι (which thing) plainly referring to Πιςυ in the verfe immediately preceding.

But not only the grammatical conftruction of the words ufed, the ideas conveyed by them, equally forbid the reception of Dr. Dodderidge's interpretation, as may appear from the Effay before referred to, and from the Appendix to that Effay, to both which *this* was intended as an introduction; but was I believe thought too *Logical* for a religious magazine.

AN ESSAY UPON THE NATURE AND USE OF ABSTRACT IDEAS.

The ideas which men are poffeffed of arife in their minds, either

I. In confequence of the action of external objects upon the corporeal fenfes. For the Creator of mankind has fo formed the human frame, that the various works of creation, i. e. external objects, can produce changes in the *ftate* (though not in the *nature)* both of our *faculties* and *difpofitions,* by means of our corporeal fenfes; changes in which our *power* of choice, i. e. our will, has no concern : and the involuntary, i. e. the unfought information arifing from thefe effects of external objects upon our *senses*, make a very great and a very useful part of our knowledge.

Or they are,

II. Modifications of these original ideas, produced by means of the *operations* of the internal powers of the mind, in consequence of the *action* of the will.

The *first* information received by human creatures, is plainly that which is received from the *effects*, or as it is sometimes called, from the *impressions* of external objects upon the senses of the body, that is, as Mr. Locke would say, from sensation. Now I call every information arising from a *single* effect produced upon the senses by an external object, an *original* perception, and the effect itself produced upon the mind by this *original* perception, I call an *idea* : so that ideas are *not* perceptions, but the effects, or consequences of perceptions, of whatever sort these perceptions are : and in proof of *this* difference, it may be observed, that although the human mind has a power of recalling its ideas, which power we call *memory*, and the exercise of this power, recollection, yet men cannot recall the *actual* perception received by the senses ; for if they could, the effects of the actions of external objects might be rendered *perpetual* ; pain and pleasure derived from the senses would become capable of endless repetition, or rather of endless continuation ; one smelling bottle might serve a nation, and the dog would cry at the sound of that bell, which now he only runs from, through apprehension of the whip which is tied to it.

But though the mind has little or no power over its *original*, or *transmitted* perceptions, it has great power over its own ideas : and though it cannot *create* an idea, *originally*, from itself, independent of the actions of ex-

ternal objects ; yet juft as men cannot *create* matter,
but can only alter the form and fize of that which is
created ; can feparate it, or join it together in various
ways ; fo they can alfo modify their ideas : can by comparing them difcern the differences between them ; can
feparate from each other fuch as have been *fuggefted together*, as it were in company : and can *combine together*, fuch as have been *fuggefted feparately*. But thefe
ideas *thus* modified, neither are, nor can be fuggefted
to the mind by external objects, through the immediate action of the fenfes ; they owe their origin to the voluntary operations of the intellectual powers, vet thefe
ideas thus modified are capable of various relations ;
and while the ideas remain unchanged, thefe relations
remain unalterable. Matter indeed can, and often
does admit of changes, which may not be perceptible
at the time they take place, though difcoverable after-
wards, but our ideas admit of no imperceptible changes.
When then we *feiect* certain ideas from amongft others,
for our contemplation and confideration ; and remove
from our attention certain other ideas which were received along with them, the ideas fo felected are called
abftract, i. e. abftracted ideas, that is, ideas taken from
fuch as accompanied them when they entered into the
mind.

It feems to me that Mr. Locke fpeaks of this and
other operations of the mind, as if they were the effects
of much, and mature reflexion. But like words, and
what is more, the peculiar force of words, they appear
to be learned, by intercourfe and experience. I have
known a child perfectly acquainted with the expreffive
force of language, before it was able to fpeak plain, fay
" I ownt"—" I ownt"—*I fay* I ownt ; and upon being corrected, fay " I'ill—I'ill—*indeed* I'ill." From
perceiving feveral objects of the fame kind, children

H

ſoon learn the nature and uſe of numbers, and quickly diſcern that one is not two, and that one and two put together do not make four. From obſerving the different ſize and colour of birds they ſoon learn to include them under the general name ; and thus they begin to exerciſe the power of abſtraction, before they are able to underſtand the nature and the uſe of it, and without knowing what a ſelf-evident propoſition is, they perceive clearly that the whole is greater than a part, and when half an apple is offered to them, wiſely cry for the whole. It is in ways like theſe that mankind learn to exert their various powers, and to exerciſe their various faculties of body and mind.

Abſtract ideas may relate either to

I. Quantity.————Under the idea of quantity, I comprehend whatever is capable of meaſure—as lines—ſurfaces—ſolids : and it may be angles—ratios—numbers. It will readily be underſtood, that by meaſures, is meant meaſures ſui generis. The purpoſe of this kind of abſtraction is to obtain *general* truths, reſpecting different kinds of magnitude. Theſe truths are the ſubjects of all mathematical reaſoning.

When mathematicians prepare ideas for the diſcovery of what is called mathematical truth by abſtraction, the ideas removed from conſideration, are (as in all caſes of abſtract ideas) univerſally ſuch, as have any connexion with *real* exiſtence, that is, ſuch as are matters of ſenſe. So the ſolids have *no* ſubſtance—the plain ſurfaces *no* thickneſs—the lines *no* breadth—the points *no* magnitude—the figures *no* ſize. The triangles ſuppoſe are neither equilateral—equicrural—ſcalene—acute, right, or obtuſe angled, &c. The knowledge acquired is *general* knowledge, and therefore is only *ideal.* Draw the figures upon paper, cut them out of any substance whatever, and the proposition (as referred to such figures) is *not* true. The *assumed* circumstances are wholly arbitrary, and upon these arbitrary circumstances, the truth to be demonstrated intirely depends.

Having thus ascertained the ideas, whose relations they propose to investigate, they usually proceed to lay down what they call postulates, that is, requisitions to admit, not the possibility of making a solid, which has *no* substance; a surface, which has *no* thickness, or of drawing a line, which has *no* breadth, and making a point, which has *no* size; nor yet of *conceiving* such a solid, or such a surface, line, or point, which is equally impossible; but to admit the possibility of considering a solid with regard to extension *only*; a surface merely with regard to its length and breadth; a line with regard to its length and direction, when compared with other lines, as to these circumstances; and the possibility of considering a *point* with regard to its *situation only*. A postulate then implies, that such *partial* consideration does not involve any *ideal contradiction*; such as it is to require the *whole* to be taken out of a part.

When then a mathematician proposes certain ideas for consideration, he does not say conceive a line, or lines in general, or conceive a point in general: he supposes you possessed of these ideas by *some* way or other: for such ideas are *simple* ideas, and do not admit of being *defined*: but he says conceive a line of such or such a length, or continued in such a direction : or conceive a point so and so placed, &c. As, conceive three lines of such a sort, that any two of them, taken together, may be longer than the third, and let these lines be so joined as to *include* space : or conceive a curve *returning* into *itself*, of such a sort that a point may be taken *within* the curve, at an equal distance from every part of such curve, &c. Now all thefe circumftances are matters of *choice* to him, and from ideas fo circumftanced, according to his pleafure, he can trace out various relations, and deduce various truths.

But abftract ideas may relate

II. To the circumftances which difcriminate the various forts of animate and inanimate matter from each other refpectively.—Now when we remove from our attention the peculiar ideas, which accompany the particular external objects that excite thefe ideas in our minds ; and felect for our contemplation, thofe ideas which are excited *not* by *one* fingle object only, but by a *confiderable number* of thefe objects ; that is, when we abftract *fuch* ideas as are to be found in *all* thefe objects, from thofe in which *every* individual differs from every other individual, we form a *general idea*, not indeed agreeing with any one individual, but generally defcriptive of the whole fpecies.

Therefore when we have recourfe to abftraction in order to generalize our ideas, and to rank *numbers* of particular beings under *one term* ; the ideas to be abftracted, are not matters of *arbitrary* appointment ; this abftraction muft be fo made as to *include* thofe ideas only, in which *all* the particular beings to be comprehended under this *one* term agree ; rejecting from our confideration all the reft. Thus if you chufe to generalize the term bird, and, inftead of applying it to one particular individual, you wifh to extend it to, and to comprehend under it every *fort* of birds, whatever be their fhape, fize, colour, &c. ; you muft felect fuch circumftances as belong to the *whole kind*, and to this fpecies of living creatures *only*. It will not therefore be fufficient to defcribe birds as fuch creatures which *lay eggs* fuppofe, becaufe tortoifes and alligators lay eggs ; nor will it be fufficient to defcribe them as fuch living things as fly, for then you would exclude oftriches, and take in flying fifhes and infects; but if you defcribe them as having two legs and two wings, and perhaps you may add feathers, though I know not whether bats are not covered with hair, your *general* defcription may be exact.

As the fubject of one fort of abftraction is that from whence we derive the different relations of quantity, or magnitude, in *general* ; and another fort that by which we are enabled to make a general arrangement of beings, whether animate, or inanimate, in order to comprehend great numbers under one *generic* term, the fubject of the next fort of abftraction is that which comprehends,

III. Such abftract ideas as arife from the confideration of the actions of *intelligent* and *refponfible* beings : and by generalizing fuch actions we arrive at thofe *moral* ideas called, *mixed modes*.

Now I call beings refponfible beings, who are capable of *receiving*, and alfo of *difcerning* the *fitnefs*, *propriety* and *rectitude* of fuch *rules* of action as may be given unto them. Animals are capable of having their actions governed in fome degree, and in an imperfect manner, by the application of *immediate* pain. The horfe that is troublefome to the fmith that fhoes him, may be reftrained from his offenfive tricks, by a great knock on his ribs with the hammer, or a good kick on the guts ; but this correction affords *no* inftruction to the team which is paffing by at the inftant. Man alone of all creatures that we are acquainted with, is capable of perceiving the *fitnefs*, *propriety* and *rectitude* of that rule of action which God his Creator has given him, by whatever way it may be made known to him.

We become acquainted with the *mere* actions of men, in the same way as we become acquainted with the actions of all other creatures, or with the nature of, and changes in the material world about us. And we are called upon by that mental constitution which God has given us, to consider the *nature* of our own actions, for the direction of our *own* conduct just in the same way, and just as much, as we are called upon by the possession of sight, to direct our steps ; because to what purpose are the manifold gifts of God bestowed upon us, but that we may avail ourselves of all the benefits from them which they can afford us. For this is the *peculiar* advantage of intelligence.

God then has made men responsible creatures ; and all those relations which intercede between agents and their actions, that is, between men and their conduct, arise from, or are built upon this responsibility ; and upon these relations *all moral* character is founded. But character is not discoverable from, or to be attributed to a few detached actions. It arises from the *general cast*, or tenor of our dispositions, and these can only be collected from the *general cast* and *tenor* of our actions; that is, from our usual and customary conduct. Known indeed to God are all our dispositions, even *before* they proceed to *intention* ; but man seeth not as God seeth, and can only judge of the *internal* dispositions, that is of the character, from the *outward* conduct.

Now it is *intention alone* which constitutes the difference between the voluntary operations of intelligent agents, and the *casual* effects proceeding from irrational creatures, or from those of inanimate matter. Because intention implies a *desire* of producing certain *foreseen* effects ; and the intentions of intelligent agents can only be collected by the *occasional* circumstances of each particular action : juſt as their *permanent* diſpoſitions can alone be diſcovered by the *conſtant tenor* of their conduct ; and as the preſence or abſence of intention can only be collected by the occaſional circumſtances of each *particular* action, ſo the *nature* of theſe intentions, that is, the *morality*, the rectitude, or depravity, their title to approbation, or abhorrence can likewiſe alone be known by a conſideration of theſe *ſame* occaſional cir-cumſtances, of mens' reſpective actions. For the more ready communication of knowledge, men have genera-lized theſe ideas reſpecting their various diſpoſitions, and the conduct ariſing from theſe diſpoſitions, juſt as they generalize many other ideas, reducing them into ſorts, and giving names to the *various* ſorts ; names, not ex-preſſive of the particular diſpoſitions, or particular con-duct of *ſingle* individuals, but of *all* diſpoſitions, and *all* conduct of a *ſimilar* ſort, to be found in men of all ages and nations : and theſe ideas, thus joined together un-der, or (as Mr. Locke would ſay) by one name, are uſually called *mixed modes*.

Thus, we call contentment a *habit* of reſtraining our uneaſineſs under the *want* of ſome good, patience a ha-bit of reſtraining our uneaſineſs under the *preſſure* of ſome evil. Thus again, fortitude is a habit of bearing *preſent* evil, for the ſake of future good. Self-denial an habit of reſtraining *innocent* deſires, that *blamable* ones may be more eaſily governed. Benevolence an habitual deſire of promoting the good of others, generoſity an habit of promoting the good of others at the *expence* of the *pro-moter*, and ſoon.

Now theſe mixed modes have their foundation, like all other abſtract ideas, in that conſtitution, or frame which God has appointed in this world. (See Butler's Sermons, edit. iii. p. 47.) that is to ſay, in the relations of human creatures to each other, or to other intelligent beings : and this conſtitution is *permanent*, or, according to the ufual way of fpeaking, nature is always the *fame*: that is, certain *forts* of difpofitions, i. e. certain *fimilar* difpofitions, (for by *forts* of things we always mean *fimilar* things) are to be found in great numbers of individuals. It never happens that fome difpofitions, which *once* generally prevailed in confiderable portions of mankind, ceafe to be found in the human race. The *general* ideas taken from thefe difpofitions, or from the conduct fuch difpofitions naturally, i. e. *ufually* produce, like all other abftract ideas, are *fixed* and *invariable*; and *thefe* ideas muft have been generally included under *thofe* names, which have been commonly annexed to fuch ideas; which names are to be found in the languages of almoft all nations. For it is to be prefumed, that writers no more ufe their words, without any meaning annexed to fuch words, than men ever talk a language to others, which the fpeakers know is not underftood by the hearers. As then the ideas annexed to the *words ufed* by *writers* to exprefs mixed modes, muft be *fixed* and *invariable*; it is not poffible that fuch expreffions fhould *wholly* change their meaning : e. g. juftice cannot fignify injuftice, or cruelty humanity, generofity felfifhnefs, profufenefs parfimony, or truth falfhood. In enumerating then the ideas which enter into mixed modes ufed by any writers, we muft not include amongft them fuch ideas, with which it is impoffible thefe writers fhould be acquainted. Thus we find the word virtue ufed by the Grecian and Roman moralifts, but if you fay that virtue confifts in conformity of the human conduct to the will of God, you put into your definition of virtue an idea, with which it is impoffible that thefe moralifts fhould be acquainted. Becaufe obedience to the will of God, implies a *knowledge* of the *unity* of God : but the unity of God, was either not known, or not acknowledged, by the profeffors of Polytheifm. This definition of virtue then feems liable to the same objection, as that of Dr. Paley, (see the second set of Essays by T. Ludlam, Essay viii.) It involves ideas, which neither were, nor could be known to many, who were no strangers to this mixed mode. For moral modes are founded upon the *common* principles of our *common nature*, and therefore must lie within the bounds of *natural* knowledge. They cannot have any connexion with such knowledge as is plainly supernatural, however desirable this latter sort of knowledge may become from circumstances, which although foreseen, certainly *could not be intended* ; because to suppose a deficiency of knowledge *intended*, is to overturn *all* those ideas, which men are enabled to collect, and which it seems was the *design* of their Creator, that they *should* collect from his works, concerning his *nature* and his *dispositions*.

But it is not merely to those abstract ideas which regard the relations, that either make part of, or arise from, that constitution which God has appointed us, that our attention is necessary, if we would attain *precise* knowledge : we must never forget that *these* ideas are not received from *any one* particular object, like *those* of sense, but that they are wholly *factitious*, the mere creation of the mind, formed only for the purpose of giving readiness to the verbal communication of knowledge. Abstract terms are nothing but an invention to assist human language : These terms must therefore never be used as if they were expressive of objects really existing ; because when general terms, which are only expressive of abstract ideas, are used as if such terms were applicable to *real* existence, that is, to such objects for which we have the *testimony* of our *senses*, much confusion must arise from this improper and injudicious application, as the following instances will abundantly shew :—

I

" To fathers in their private families," says Bishop Horne, in his Discourse upon the Origin of Civil Government, " *nature* has given *supreme* power."—Nature! —The God of nature surely! The term nature is a *mere* word: the mark not of any particular, but of a general or abstract idea, to which *no precise* meaning *is*, or can be annexed. It refers to that *usual* and *established mode* of acting, which God has thought proper to employ in his work of creation : and when we talk of the gifts of nature, we mean those gifts of God, those powers, faculties, qualities, qualifications which *he* bestows indiscriminately, though perhaps not equally, upon all the various *species* of beings *respectively :* and these powers, faculties, qualifications, qualities, when referred to each respective species, are called the *nature* of that species : when writers then apply this general, or abstract term, as if it stood for some *particular* matter, and fancy they affirm some thing, they in reality affirm nothing, no *particular* truth. But general truths have no relation to—are no marks of real existence ; and so the *same general term*, which represents to the mind no *one* thing in the universal world, *equally* serves the pious Bishop of Norwich, and the Infidei defenders of Atheism, (see Dr. Paley's Natural Theology, page 446,) for the support of their respective systems.

So again, when Mr. Robinson, a celebrated gospel minister affirms, that the *same* nature which sinned, atoned, (Script. Charact. Vol. iii. p. 29, or 35) and when Dr. Hawker, a no less celebrated gospel minister affirms the direct contrary, (see his Essay upon the Divinity of Christ, page 8,) that the *same* nature which sinned, did *not* atone, for that the *divine* nature, (which *could not* sin) atoned ; neither one nor the other of these two great divines, was able to perceive that they had no ideas to their words ; for both divine and human nature are merely abstract terms, and could no more atone, than they could talk. It would have been juft as intelligible, and juft as wife to fay that human nature might be punifhed, might be hanged fuppofe, or tranfported to Botany Bay, or be whipped at the cart's-tail. Take another inftance of this literary legerdemain. "The Holy Spirit," (fays Mr. Cruden, fee his Concordance, word Spirit) " is called a perfon," (not in Scripture furely) "becaufe whatever *belongs* to perfon, as to underftand, to will, to give, to call, to do, to fubfift of himfelf, doth agree to the fpirit," and he adds, " who appeared in a vifible fhape." But furely Mr. Cruden would no more call the Dove a perfon, or the fiery tongues, than he would call the flame of fire in the bufh, which Mofes faw, a perfon, Deut. iv. 12, 13. By perfon Mr. Cruden plainly means the *general* idea of living being; though this is by no means the common idea of perfon; for if perfon means any thing, it means a vifible human form; and if it does not, it would be equally proper to talk of the perfons of animals.

In a note of Dr. Hey's Norrifian Lectures, Vol. ii. p. 275, we are told that Bifhop Pearfon fays, " God died for us," and Dr. Hey adds, that the Bifhop means that *perfon* died. Here the idea annexed to the word perfon is not the idea of *being in general*, but that of a particular fort, which we call (and underftand by it human) body: and it might with equal propriety have been affirmed, no lefs than of perfon, that prefence (another general, or abftract idea) died. With equal want of *diftinct* ideas, we are told in the fame Note (what is indeed often faid by divines, but I think never in Scripture) that *Chrift has two natures*, in *one* perfon. Afcertain but the ideas conveyed by the words nature and perfon, and the propofition will be found utterly *unintelligible*. The word perfon conveys only an abftract, or general idea; we do not underftand by this term the idea of body, or of living body in *general*, for then we might fpeak of the

perſons of animals: ſtill leſs can it be ſuppoſed to
mean, the ſame as it meant by the word ſpirit; for the
idea annexed to the word ſpirit is merely negative, (ſee
an Eſſay upon the Epiſtle to the Romans, printed in
the Orthodox Churchman's Magazine for January,
1803,) and when we ſpeak of ſpirits, it means, if it
means any thing, that ſpirits have *no* perſons; i. e. no
viſible form, as men have; becauſe the word perſon is
only uſed to expreſs the *general* form of the human body,
that is, a form which has *no* ſize, colour, &c. and therefore
the word perſon in general, neither does, nor can imply any thing which really exiſts, that is, which is the
object of ſenſe; becauſe we neither have, nor can have,
any *ſenſible* knowledge of whatever exiſts without colour,
ſize, &c. We may indeed *believe* that ſuch things exiſt, but *faith* is *not knowledge*; and it is never ſuppoſed
that the word perſon conveys what is only an object of
faith. Divines indeed have applied this word to the
Supreme Being, but unqueſtionably without any idea, *

* A remarkable inſtance of this miſapplication we have in the
23d Chapter of Dr. Paley's Natural Theology, written expreſsly
upon what he calls the *Perſonality* of God, as if *it* was an attribute of
the divine nature.

At p. 429, 2d edit. The Doctor ſays contrivance proves the Perſonality of the Deity. He ſhould have ſaid, the *exiſtence* of a con-
triver, in oppoſition to thoſe who talk of nature, &c. as capable of
ſupplying the *place* of an *intelligent* agent. He goes on, now *that*
(being I ſuppoſe) *which* can deſign muſt be a *perſon*. If he had ſaid,
muſt be a *living* agent, he would have expreſſed himſelf more clearly. For any idea which we can form of *perſon*, has no more *neceſſary*
connection with activity, or intelligence, than activity, or intelligence have, with the *exerciſe* of them, being connected with objects
of ſight—it is alſo not unuſual to ſpeak of *dead* perſons. He further
ſays, the capacities of contrivance and deſign imply conſciouſneſs
and thought; and therefore *conſtitute perſonality*. If he had ſaid theſe
capacities imply an *intelligent* agent, he would have expreſſed himſelf ſtill more clearly: and if this is not his meaning he ſhould have
told us *what* is; becauſe the words perſon, and perſonality are not
applicable to all living beings, as we have juſt obſerved. For the

and it has been done only to fupport an *unintelligible* notion; and fo the greek words χαρακτὴρ τῆς ὑποϛασιως have

abftract idea annexed to the word perfon, is made up of a vifible human form, unattended with any of the particular ideas of great, or
fmall, tall or fhort, corpulent or thin, fair or black, frefh coloured
or pale, ugly or handfome, &c. The word perfon therefore when
applied to a particular being, means, if it means any thing, an object of fenfe. Nobody talks of the *perfon* of the *foul.* To fay then
that in *whatever* the *mind refides* is a *perfon,* and that the *feat* of intelligence is a *perfon,* is humana ad Deos transferre; is to ufe his own
words a perverfion of language, for it is to ufe words without ideas.
Becaufe what are we to underftand by a mind *refiding?* and what by
the feat of the intellect? To apply fuch ideas to God, is, it fhould
feem, to fuppofe that he has parts; otherwife why the diftinction of
where the mind *is,* and where it is not? And to apply the word
perfon to him, is furely, if we have any ideas to our words, to fuppofe him an object of fenfe, in direct contradiction to Scripture, Job
xxiii. 8, 9. For what other reafon can be given, why the word
perfon is never applied to the human mind, which alone has the ca-
pacity of thought, and confcioufnefs, and therefore of contrivance
and defign? And if the application of the word perfon to God, is
not to fuppofe him an object of fenfe, *what* is the *difference* between
a perfon and an intelligent being? Perhaps higher orders of intelligent beings may be qualified to difcern more of the Deity, as well
as more of his works, than is permitted to men: but we neither have,
nor under our prefent circumftances can have any more notion (unlefs
the Lord imparts new faculties to us, as he did to the prophet and
his fervant, 2 Kings vi. 17,) of this perception than we have of the
perceptions, which St. Paul had in the third heaven. *Particular*
language therefore in thefe cafes is utterly inapplicable. To have
faid, as is very properly faid, p. 444, that contrivance implies an intelligent author of what is contrived, would have removed this juftly
exceptionable mode of fpeaking.

It is well obferved, at p. 446, that the *force* of the reafoning, (the
reafoning *itfelf* he fhould have faid) is frequently funk by our taking
up with *mere* names. Thus nature means *not* an *agent,* but the *order,*
according to which the author of that nature acts; and it is abfurd to
afcribe to the order of things, a power of producing that order: the
things themfelves muft *firft* be produced, before that order can take
place; for order means only a regular arrangement; but to arrange
is the proper work of an intelligent agent, becaufe it implies choice,
and choice implies volition, but volition is only the property of living
beings. Nature, order, mechanifm, are abftract ideas, but the
names of abftract ideas are never the marks of real exiftence.

been tranſlated, the expreſs image of his perſon, although the word 'υπόςασις, no more ſignifies *perſon*,
than it ſignifies *body*. But this jugling change of the
meaning has been effected by the magical operation of
ſchool divinity.—And what can be meant by the word
nature, but that ſyſtem or combination of powers, diſ-

It is truly obſerved, p. 458, that perſons who ſpeak of abſtract
ideas, ſuch as nature, order, mechaniſm, &c. as cauſes of objects
which exiſt, mean to *deny*, or *ſet aſide* the operation of a particular
perſonal intelligence ; that is to ſay, the exertions of an intending,
and contriving mind; what is called, p. 462, a deſigning mind, and
p. 464, an intelligent deſigning Creator. Now when we ſpeak of
an intending, contriving, deſigning mind, we talk of what we *clearly* underſtand, as *far* as we underſtand, though it may not be what
we *perfectly*, i. e. intirely comprehend : artificers, and architects,
are terms familiar with us ; but what idea are we to annex to a *perſonal* intelligence, i. e. a *perſonal mind ?* Deſign muſt have had a deſigner ; is any thing *more* meant, when it is ſaid, that ſuch deſigner
muſt have been a *perſon ?* If there is, *what* is it ? If there is not,
why uſe the word ? I am apt to ſuſpect that names like this, to uſe
Dr. Paley's words, *refer* us to *nothing ;* excite no idea, convey a
ſound to the ear but no more.—Vox et præteria nihil.

At p. 475, we are told that it is one of the advantages of revelation, that it introduces the Deity to human apprehenſions under an
idea more *perſonal*, more *determinate*, more within its compaſs than
the theology of nature. To be ſure if we conſider natural theology
alone, we learn little more than that a wiſe, good, and powerful Being is the author and preſerver of the univerſe. It is from revelation
that we learn the moſt particular (which make the idea, if not more
perſonal, certainly more determinate) and therefore the moſt *important relations* in which God ſtands to us, as our ſupreme governor,
and our judge; and it is from His word alone that we become acquainted with Him as our redeemer, and our ſanctifier : But if theſe
ideas are more *perſonal*, it is becauſe Chriſt is *appointed* to be our
judge, John v. 22. Acts xvii. 31; and we are further told, John
v. 27, the reaſon of this appointment. But though revelation ſhews
us more of the divine goodneſs, it affords us no clearer, nor any further conceptions of the divine power, than we can gather from His
works, much leſs does it add any thing to our knowledge of what is
here called His *perſonality :* of that, ſo far as we can have any idea to
the word, we underſtand not a whit more than we did before, that is
—*juſt nothing.*

politions, qualifications, &c. which the Creator of all
things has been pleafed to appoint to the productions of
his own will ? And then how is it poffible that any
thing can have *two* natures. But thefe divines tell us,
what the Scriptures no where do, " that Chrift has two
natures, the divine, and the human." But becaufe
Chrift exercifed powers far fuperior to thofe of men,
Luke xi. 20. John iii. 2. are we therefore to afcribe to
him the *underived* poffeffion of fuch power, without *exprefs* authority for fuch afcription from holy writ. We
fhould be careful to diftinguifh between the *weak* and
uncertain inferences of human reafon, and the *clear* and
pofitive declarations of divine revelation, in fubjects
upon which we cannot poffibly acquire any other information than what is imparted to us by God himfelf.
And how can we afcribe the divine nature to any being
unlefs we are clearly acquainted with the powers, and
difpofitions of that nature ? Men have frequently exercifed powers far fuperior to thofe ufually allotted to the
human race, but whoever thought of afcribing the divine nature to them. St. Peter exhorts his converts to
the practice of the moral virtues, that they may become,
not poffeffors, but partakers of the divine nature ; i. e.
may refemble in their meafure, the great author and pof-
feffor of all moral goodnefs, Matt. v. 48. Luke vi. 35, 36.
Matt. v. 45. And as we cannot have any foundation,
unlefs from revealed information, to afcribe the divine
nature to any being but the Supreme, fo we learn from
that information, that there are parts of the divine nature, which either *could* not, or *do* not, 2. Tim. vi. 16.
Matt. xxiv. 36. Mark xiii. 32. belong to any other being but the Supreme. And let not eager, ignorant zeal
take fire, as if any thing which is here faid is any dimi-
nution of the glory, or any difparagement to the honour
of the Redeemer. However little we may underftand of
the relations in which Chrift ftands to God, we *clearly*

understand those in which he stands to us. We certainly know that he was our Creator, and is the governor and preserver of this world, and therefore has a claim to every duty and service appendant upon those relations, as well as to all those which arise from his character as our Redeemer. And his most earnest followers would have done better, to have received *implicitly* without attempting to *explain* what we are utterly unable to understand: thus *disgracing* themselves, and dishonouring him, by esteeming it possible that the fruits of ignorance and folly could be acceptable to him.

AN ESSAY UPON THE DIFFERENCE BETWEEN MATHEMATICAL AND MORAL PROOF.

Few writers attend to the difference between such proof as is applicable to mathematical, and such as is applicable to moral truth. Hence we often hear of *such* truths being *demonstrated*, as are utterly incapable of this *sort* of proof. Mr. Locke himself seems inclined to think both sorts of truth equally capable of demonstration in his Essay upon the Human Understanding, B. III. Chap. xi. Sect. 16. and B. IV. Chap. iii. Sect. 18. Chap. xii. Sect. 8. But had he attended to the different *nature* of mathematical and moral ideas, and also to *that* of the relations interceding between each respective sort, he would probably have been of a different opinion. Ideas are the *materials* of *all* our knowledge ; and the *relations* interceding between these *ideas*, determine the *species* of our knowledge.

By ideas I understand,

I. *Original* sensations arising in the mind in consequence of the actions of *external* objects upon the corporeal senses.—Or

II. *Voluntary* modifications of these ideas so received, in consequence of the operation of our *internal* powers.

If we consider the different ways by which we become possessed of our ideas, we may perhaps discover more accurately the *nature* of these ideas, the *relations* which arise from their nature, and also the species of proof applicable to each respective sort, as depending upon *this* nature, and *these* relations.

All our original sensations are admitted into the mind through our various senses. Such as are derived from *sight*, are properly called *images*. A representation of the appearance of the object, is formed in some manner within the mind. Such sensations as spring from our *other* senses are called more properly *ideas*. No resemblance attends the perceptions from which these ideas rise. Hence it follows that though *all images* are *ideas*, yet *all ideas* are *not images*; and also that images are, and must be, ideas of particular objects. There can be no such thing as *general*, or *abstract images*, though there may be *general* or *abstract* ideas. For the mind has certain powers over its ideas, and can at pleasure, compare, combine, separate, or recall them ; and in consequence of these powers can produce various *modifications* of them, for the more *ready* acquisition, or communication of knowledge. Thus by abstracting *all* those circumstances in which a number of particular ideas *differ* from each other, and retaining all those circumstances in which they *agree*, the mind *forms* what are called general, or abstract ideas. But these *general* or *abstract* ideas are never presented to, or produced in the mind, like our *original* perceptions, by causes from *without*, or

K

foreign to itself : they are the *voluntary formation* of the mind ; and that they are so, is plain ; because the mind can form ideas of *this* kind, which are more or less general Thus, bird is a more general idea than sparrow, and creature than bird, and being than creature. So again solid bodies consist of three dimensions, viz. length, breadth and thickness. By abstracting the idea of thickness, and retaining those of length and breadth, we form the idea of a plain surface : by abstracting from the idea of surface its breadth, we obtain the idea of a line ; and by still further abstracting from our idea of a line, its length we arrive at, the idea of a *mathematical* point.

The exertion of this power we call the *act* of conceiving ; though it may be that we understand no more of this faculty, than we do of that which we call recollection. It is nevertheless a real power, and is plainly unconnected with that species of ideas which we call images. For blind persons are capable, in consequence of *this* power, of understanding the various relations of lines, surfaces and solids, and also the mathematical laws of optics, though how much they know of colours may be collected from the reply of that blind person, who said he supposed that scarlet resembled the *sound* of a trumpet ; nor is it at all likely that such persons can by any means acquire that species of ideas which we call images. Mr. Locke mentions an inquiry made by his friend Mr. Molineux, B. II. Chap. ix. Sect. 8. whether a blind person who was acquainted with the different properties of the sphere and cube, might not, upon the recovery of sight, distinguish by the use of it, one of these solids from the other ? But had Mr. Molineux considered that the visible appearances of bodies depend *wholly* upon the different degrees of light and shade, and upon the angles made by the visual ray with the various bounding lines of such objects, both which can *only* be

suggefted through the *eye*, he might have fafely concluded that fuch a perfon could not diftinguifh by fight
only, triangles from fquares.* Hence it is plain that
images can *only* be received by *fight* ; that they neither
are, nor can be received by the touch, even when they
refpect the boundaries of extenfion, or of fpace, i. e. of
figure. Mathematical ideas, therefore, like all abftract
ideas, are unqueftionably *formed* by the mind, in a
manner perhaps inexplicable, the fact however cannot
be doubted. *Conceive* fuch and fuch ideas is the language refpecting their formation. They are therefore,
and muft be the *fame* in all mankind, becaufe they are
formed by *prefcription.* Their formation is a matter of
command, not of *choice.* Every idea prefcribed muft be
taken in, not one can be left out confiftent with the
truths propofed to be eftablifhed, for it is the relations
of *given* ideas to fpeak in mathematical language, which
are to be afcertained. The idea of a triangle is precifely
the *fame* in every mind. It is compofed of the ideas of
three ftrait lines, joined together in fuch a manner as to
include fpace. So the idea of a circle is exactly *alike* in
every man. It is the idea of a curve returning into itfelf, of fuch a fort that a point can be taken *within* the
curve, *equidiftant* from *every part* of the curve. A ftrait
line drawn through this point, and continued to each
fide of the curve is called a diameter. Every perfon who
forms the idea of fuch a curve, fees *immediately*, and *intuitively*, that the diameter is, and muft *neceffarily* be
double the radius. Again the relations fubfifting between thefe ideas, is, and muft be *immutable.* With
ever be the proportions and inclinations of the fides of
triangles to each other, the three angles of every triangle
will invariably be equal to two right angles : Whatever the length of the diameter of any circle, it will al-

* A matter of a fimilar fort is related in Addifon's Tatler.

ways be double the length of the radius : And so of every mathematical proposition. Mathematical truth are therefore *neceſſary* truths.

The caſe with *moral* truths is totally different. The ideas from whoſe relations theſe truths ariſe, do not ſpring like mathematical truths from *preſcribed* conceptions : for mixed modes are the voluntary combination of the mind that forms them. The ideas themſelves, of which theſe modes conſiſt, are not *faſtitious*, as mathematical ideas are ; it is the *combination* of them into *one complex* idea which is alone *faſtitious* ; for this combination is perfeſtly arbitrary, Locke, B. II. Chap. xxii. It depends upon the *will* of him who makes it, and who *chooſes* what ideas he will combine together. But the formation of mathematical ideas, ſo far as regards the nature of them, does not depend upon the will of him who forms them : this nature is aſcertained by the *original* formation of them, in conſequence of a *preſcribed* conception, and therefore admits of no variation. Now by demonſtration we mean a *general* proof; viz. one that holds true of *all* the ideas of one ſort. Thus what is true of one triangle, or one circle, is true of all other triangles, and all other circles whatever, however they may differ from each other, and ſo of every other figure. But the truth of propoſitions conſiſting of mixed modes, muſt depend not upon the ideas themſelves, but upon this *arbitrary* combination of them ; and men rarely agree, either in the ideas they aſtually join together, or in determining what ideas it is *expedient* to join. So moral obligation is a mixed mode, but what very different definitions are given of it ? That is to ſay, what different ideas are combined together by different perſons under this name ? ſo different indeed as to occaſion great variety in the concluſions reſpeſting it. But this is not all. For if demonſtration was applicable to moral truths, the concluſion *muſt* be *neceſſary*. Becauſe

we mean by demonftration that proof only, whofe conclufion is *neceffary*. But if the conclufions of proofs refpecting human actions were neceffary (and moral truths
refpect human actions only) there would be an end of
moral agency, becaufe liberty is the ground of all moral
agency; but neceffity and liberty are inconfiftent : for
by liberty I mean the *power* of choice, and by neceffity
the *want* of this power. Where matters *muft* be what
they *are*, choice can have no place. Could you *demon-
ftrate* that men *muft* obey God ; i. e. that they could *not
poffibly* difobey him, obedience would ceafe to be acceptable. Men would be mere machines. There are indeed who talk of *moral neceffity*; they might as well talk
of neceffary liberty. The ideas are utterly inconfiftent,
as inconfiftent as a ftrait curve.

FINIS.

THOEMMES PRESS

BOOKS RELATING TO JOHN LOCKE

(Second series)

FOX BOURNE, H.R.: The Life of John Locke
[1876]   *In Two Volumes*   508pp & 588pp
ISBN 1 85506 113 9   **£88.00**

KING, Lord Peter: The Life of John Locke, with extracts from his correspondence. A new edition with considerable additions   [1830]
In Two Volumes   462pp & 530pp
ISBN 1 85506 114 7   **£88.00**

LOCKE, John: Discourses: Translated from [Pierre] Nicole's Essays   [1828]   274pp
ISBN 1 85506 115 5   **£32.00**

LUDLAM, Thomas: Logical   Tracts; comprising Observations and Essays illustrative of Mr Locke's Treatise upon the Human Understanding   [1790]   114pp
ISBN 1 85506 116 3   **£28.00**

MORELL, Thomas: Notes and Annotations on Locke on the Human Understanding   [1794]
ISBN 1 85506 117 1   130pp   **£30.00**

PERRONET, Vincent: A Second Vindication of Mr Locke   [1738]   158pp   *With a new Introduction by John Yolton, Rutgers University*
ISBN 1 85506 118 X   **£34.00**

Books relating to John Locke (Second series)
6 titles   £300 the set   ISBN 1 85506 119 8

•CUSTOMERS IN JAPAN Please note that distribution in Japan of all books in these Reprint Series is exclusive to Kinokuniya Company of Tokyo and all orders should be placed with them.   (P.T.O.)

THOEMMES PRESS

BOOKS RELATING TO JOHN LOCKE

(First series)

CARROLL, William: A Dissertation upon the Tenth Chapter of the Fourth Book of Mr Locke's Essay Concerning Humane Understanding [1706] *With a new Introduction by John Yolton*
ISBN 1 85506 010 8   324pp   **£35.00**

FORSTER, Thomas: Original Letters of John Locke, Algernon Sydney and Lord Shaftesbury [1847]   298pp
ISBN 1 85506 011 6   **£32.00**

LARDNER, Dionysius: A Series of Lectures on Locke's Essay [1824]   98pp
With a new Introduction by Peter Alexander
ISBN 1 85506 012 4   **£22.00**

MARION, Henri: J. Locke - Sa Vie et Son Oeuvre d'après des Documents Nouveaux [1878]
ISBN 1 85506 013 2   172pp   **£30.00**

SCHÄRER, Dr Emanuel: John Locke: Seine Verstandestheorie und Seine Lehren über Religion, Staat und Erziehung [1860]   316pp
ISBN 1 85506 014 0   **£35.00**

WATTS, Isaac: Philosophical Essays on Various Subjects [1742]   432pp
With a new Introduction by John Yolton
ISBN 1 85506 015 9   **£35.00**

WEBB, Thomas: The Intellectualism of Locke: An Essay [1857]   214pp
With a new Introduction by John Yolton
ISBN 1 85506 016 7   **£26.00**

WYNNE, John: An Abridgement of Mr Locke's Essay Concerning Human Understanding [1731] *With a new Introduction by G. A. J. Rogers*
ISBN 1 85506 017 5   396pp   **£28.00**

Books relating to John Locke (First Series)
8 titles   £243 the set   ISBN 1 85506 106 6